The Musician's Legal Companion

SECOND EDITION

Michael A. Aczon

Course Technology PTR

A part of Cengage Learning

 COURSE TECHNOLOGY
CENGAGE Learning·

Australia • Brazil • Japan • Korea • Mexico • Singapore • Spain • United Kingdom • United States

COURSE TECHNOLOGY
CENGAGE Learning™

The Musician's Legal Companion
Michael A. Aczon

Publisher and General Manager,
Course Technology PTR: Stacy L. Hiquet

Associate Director of Marketing:
Sarah Panella

Manager of Editorial Services:
Heather Talbot

Marketing Manager: Mark Hughes

Executive Editor: Mark Garvey

Project Editor: Heather Johnson

Technical Reviewer: Ron Sobel

PTR Editorial Services Coordinator:
Erin Johnson

Copy Editor: Heather Johnson

Interior Layout Tech:
ICC Macmillan Inc.

Cover Designer: Mike Tanamachi

Indexer: Larry Sweazy

Proofreader: Brad Crawford

For product information and technology assistance, contact us at
Cengage Learning Customer & Sales Support, 1-800-354-9706

For permission to use material from this text or product, submit all requests online at **cengage.com/permissions**
Further permissions questions can be emailed to
permissionrequest@cengage.com

Library of Congress Control Number: 2008920137

ISBN-13: 978-1-59863-507-2

ISBN-10: 1-59863-507-7

Course Technology
25 Thomson Place
Boston, MA 02210
USA

Cengage Learning is a leading provider of customized learning solutions with office locations around the globe, including Singapore, the United Kingdom, Australia, Mexico, Brazil, and Japan. Locate your local office at:
international.cengage.com/region

Cengage Learning products are represented in Canada by Nelson Education, Ltd.

For your lifelong learning solutions, visit **courseptr.com**

Visit our corporate website at **cengage.com**

Printed in the United States of America
1 2 3 4 5 6 7 11 10 09 08

Acknowledgments

I'd like to acknowledge the following:

Heather Johnson for your relentless editing prowess. Your accuracy, speed, and stamina are amazing. Remind me to never challenge you to a 10K race.

Ron Sobel for your brilliant, gentle, and subliminal technical editing. Your years of teaching me this business are appreciated beyond my ability to put it in writing.

Stacy and Mark for breathing second life into this book.

Chaka Khan for allowing me to use your story, wisdom, and spirit as the introduction to my book. Many artists will benefit from your willingness to share your experiences.

Mike Molenda for giving me my first opportunity to write professionally.

The numerous legal clients who have touched me over the years with your lives, passion, stories, questions, deals, and art—especially the handful of artists with whom I share the unique opportunity to change the world: Renel, Sakai, Skylark, Kevin, Wayne, Martin, and Greg. Thank you.

Abraham, Eli, and John, for sharing your music with me as only brothers can.

Evan and Lauren, the most amazing children on earth. I learn so much more from you than you will ever learn from me. Thanks for choosing our house to live in on your stop over from heaven. This might not be "The Little Prince" but I hope you read it anyway.

My traveling companion, Skylark. You are the ultimate example of the word Sputnik.

About the Author

Michael A. Aczon has practiced entertainment law and managed artists since 1983. Michael has written on the business of music for *Guitar Player* and *Electronic Musician* magazines. He was a contributing writer to the book *The Independent Working Musician* by Mary Cosola. Michael has taught music industry courses at several Northern California colleges. He lives in the San Francisco Bay Area where he enjoys family, friends, writing, music, the outdoors, and life on a daily basis.

Contents

Introduction ix

PART I
PRE-PRODUCTION   1

Chapter 1
How to Use This Book   3
Companion Questions 10

Chapter 2
A Legal Primer   11
Personal Rights 13
Property Rights 14
Trademark and Copyright 17
Contract Rights 20
Specialties 21
Companion Questions 21

PART II
THE FOUR AGREEMENTS   23

Chapter 3
Songwriting and Music Publishing Agreements   25
Creative Considerations 28
Collaboration 29
Work For Hire 32

Sources of Income. 32
The Writer-Publisher Agreement 36
  What Is Included in the Catalog? 37
  Who Owns What? 38
  Administration Rights. 39
  Songwriting Commitment 39
  Advances and Recoupments. 40
Theme Variations: Timing Your Publishing Deal 43
Reversions, Revisions, and Restrictions. 43
Sample Clearance Agreement. 45
Companion Questions. 46

Chapter 4
Recording Artist Agreements   49

Background Material 51
Exclusive versus Non-exclusive 56
Contract or Lockdown? 58
Creative Control. 59
Promotional Commitments 60
Royalties and Advances. 61
Recoupable Costs 62
Royalties Revisited 63
Alternatives: Independent Record Companies 64
Alternatives: Production Agreements. 65
Alternatives: Development Deals 65
Companion Questions. 67

Chapter 5
Artist-Management Agreements   69

Development 71
Paying the Piper 75
Packaging 77
Industry Promotion. 79
Expansion 81
The Exit Plan. 82
Major Contract Points 82
Companion Questions. 87

Chapter 6
Performance Agreements 89

Scope of Performance 91
Where and When? 92
Passing the Hat 92
Travel and Accommodations 94
Contract Riders 95
Liability to Your Audience 96
No-Show Penalties 97
Merchandising 98
Ancillary Audio Visual Products. 99
Personnel. 100
Side Musicians 101
Agents. 102
Other Personnel 103
Promoters as the "New" Major Labels 104
Companion Questions. 104

PART III
BUSINESS AS USUAL 107

Chapter 7
Business Entities 109

Going It Alone. 112
Partnerships: All for One, One for All 114
Corporations and Limited Liability Companies 115
Joint Ventures 116
Non-profit Corporations 117
Deconstruction. 118
Get It in Writing 118
Companion Questions. 124

Chapter 8
Other People's Money 125

The Five Financial Fallacies. 128
Preparing for an Investor. 130

Characterizing the Cash 133
Companion Questions. 137

Chapter 9
Dispute Resolution   139

Assess the Damage 141
Remedies. 141
Self-Help 143
Mediation 144
Arbitration 145
Small Claims Court 145
Litigation 146
Heading Off Trouble 147
Companion Questions 147

PART IV
SIDE DEALS   149

Chapter 10
Declaration of Independents: A Self-Release Checklist 151

1. Artist Agreements. 153
2. Artwork 154
3. Consignment Agreements. 154
4. Consulting Agreements 155
5. Copyright Filings 155
6. Courtesy Letters 156
7. Distribution Agreements 156
8. Manufacturing and Printing Agreements 158
9. Master Licenses for Compilations. 158
10. Mechanical Licenses 159
11. Money Agreements 159
12. Musician/Vocalist/Model Releases 160
13. Music Publishing 160
14. Performance Rights Organizations 161
15. Producer Agreements 161
16. Promotion Agreements 162
17. Publicity Campaign Agreements 163

18. Samples 163
19. Studio Agreements 165
20. Trademarks 165
Conclusion. 166

Chapter 11
Distribution and Promotions Agreements   167

A Distribution Primer 167
Physical versus Digital Products 169
Physical Distribution Contract Points 170
Digital Distribution Contract Points 173
Promotions Agreements. 175

Chapter 12
Care and Feeding of Your Entertainment Lawyer   179

Lawyer Shopping 179
Maintenance 180
Specialties Within a Specialty. 184

Epilogue: Lessons Learned   189

Surround Yourself with Talent. 189
The Artist Is Your Access 190
Don't Wear Out Your Welcome 190
Prepare Yourself Before Diving into the Industry 191
Keep Learning and Teach by Example. 192
Take Some Chances 192
Your Chosen Family Is Everything 193

Glossary   195

Index   201

Introduction

About the time I was wrapping up this book, I attended a lecture by Chaka Khan, an R&B legend whose career has spanned over three decades. Khan recorded a number of multiplatinum recordings that topped the industry charts and earned a variety of industry accolades, including the coveted Grammy® Award. She was addressing a lecture hall made up largely of young artists hoping to become internationally recognized stars one day, too. She was determined to let them know what lies ahead as they pursue their places in the music industry. Her message was clear, and her passion was evident.

With tears in her eyes, Khan looked deliberately into the eyes of these industry rookies as she delivered one of the finest, most concise warnings I've ever heard about traveling down any potentially dangerous path. She told the audience how, as a teenager, she was singing in a nightclub in Chicago one night when an industry executive discovered her band. A week later, her band was signed to a major label exclusive-artist agreement and recording its first album in a studio in Los Angeles. She then went on to tell the audience that she spent the next twenty years in "industry hell," which she described as a combination of being involved with the wrong people and the wrong substances, and having the business run her life. Khan told the audience that the many twists and turns in the business side of music can turn it into an unpleasant experience. It was very clear that this superstar had considered quitting the industry time and time again because of how badly the business experience was for her. She didn't quit, though. She battled on and eventually won her freedom from being locked down to a record deal about twenty years after she started.

When asked by an audience member for career advice, she replied that one of the best things young artists can do is to study law. I had to catch my breath. Chaka Khan didn't advise them to practice scales, to sing great songs, or to work on their songwriting chops. She told them that they should study law.

I couldn't agree with her more. It's because of Khan and all other artists who had experiences similar to hers that I decided, at the age of seventeen, to become a music lawyer. After more than twenty years of practicing law as a transactional entertainment lawyer, I have come to the conclusion that the structure of how musicians and lawyers interact in our industry is severely flawed. In making that statement, I'm not pointing an accusatory finger at anyone or at the industry. I'm just making an observation based on experience.

As an example, allow me to share with you a telephone call that I've received hundreds of times in the past two decades. It's a "first encounter" phone call: A musician calls me with no introduction from someone I know or no previous contact from a conference or lecture. Likely this is someone who never has spoken to a lawyer in his or her life. It goes something like this:

"Hello?"

"Hello. I got your name from [fill in the blank here: the telephone book, a legal directory, another musician]. Do you do music contracts?"

"Yes, I review and draft entertainment contracts."

"What do you charge?"

At this point, I tell the person on the other end of the line my current hourly fee and then immediately try to get an idea of the parameters or issues surrounding the deal. I'm usually cut off at this point.

"Uh...that's a lot of money.... I think I'll try someone else."

End of conversation. It's a rocky first impression at best, but one that is repeated often. I found that I was not alone. When I started to work on this book, I asked both musicians and lawyers about their first encounters with each other. More often than not, some variation of that call is the initial impression that was exchanged. Even if the musician and lawyer started working with each other, the first impression probably stuck for a while. Although a musician's first impression of a lawyer isn't always based on financial issues, those financial concerns do bring a bit of an uncomfortable spin to how the attorney-client relationship is formed. I think it is similar to recording in a studio that charges by the hour: If you constantly have one eye on the clock because of the potential expense, it's difficult to let your ears and heart fully run free to really hear the music. The same can be said about making important decisions and agreements in your musical career.

Now, I don't intend to suggest that lawyers (or recording studios, for that matter) change their billing systems, but as I contemplated writing this book, I had to give a great deal of thought as to how to bridge the gap between two of the most important players in the entertainment industry: the musicians and the lawyers. I thought about which of my client relationships I enjoy the most. It hit me like a ton of bricks: The clients with whom I have the most fun and I am most successful representing are the ones who embrace the responsibility of their careers and, in doing so, are the ones who tend to be the most informed. By taking the time to become well informed and prepared, they are able to make the best use of my talent and time. Nothing compares to sitting with a client and a major label executive at the same table with the security of knowing that the negotiating is being done on a level playing field because both parties are equally informed about their relationship and their relative bargaining position.

My frustration about our industry is that in just about every other facet of it but law, experienced people are open and willing to allow newcomers to tag along, ask questions, and simply learn. That's why I decided to write this book.

A very dear friend and I talk about life and music as one continuous thread. We sometimes have philosophical yet practical conversations that stretch out over several months or years that meander and take on conceptual tones. One of them involved the concept of the word *sputnik*. It means traveling companion. It is the perfect word to describe how I want my book to be embraced by you, the reader. When you meet a total stranger on a walking path and strike up a conversation, sometimes you find that the two of you have something in common. It gives you something to talk about if you should both return to the path at another time. The more you talk, the more you learn from each other's experiences, ideas, and stories.

Over the years, I've taken a thousand and one walks with various people, and through those literal and figurative walks along with their accompanying talks, I have learned an awful lot about this business. It's my desire to pass on some of the lessons I've learned. I don't know you, you don't know me, but we have something in common: We love music and we want to find a way to sustain our relationship with music and those who make it. I hope to teach you what I know about this business—not simply as a lawyer, but as your legal companion. I hope that our journey is fruitful.

Pre-production

1 How to Use This Book

If you've picked up this book, there's a pretty good chance that you are a musician of some kind. Taking a very philosophical approach to the world, I suppose that one could say in some form or another, regardless of talent, proficiency, experience, or professional status, we are all musicians—singing and dancing to the melody and beat of our individual self-expression. If you accept that broad definition of the term "musician," this book can be relevant to your coveted place in the Universe as a person who shares whatever form of talent or artistry you bring to the world and to know how your work is affected by the sometimes complex workings of the law.

For purposes of simplicity, I use the term "musician" in the title and throughout this book as a loose, catchall term with the intention that it be interpreted as inclusive rather than exclusive. Allow me to give you a few examples of how using the word "musician" may dissuade some people from the benefits of learning from this book. Since vocalists are not playing a musical instrument, some people (sadly, including some vocalists themselves) do not think of themselves as musicians. While not instrumentalists, vocalists are still regarded as musicians in my mind. I treat songwriters the very same way. Many songwriters cannot read a note of music and can barely play a musical instrument; however, the multibillion-dollar music publishing industry depends on these songwriters to provide musicians with songs to share with the world. Music businesspeople in their roles as managers, agents, producers, and record label executives all perpetuate the sharing of talent, artistry, and products created by musicians; so for purposes of using this book, I consider them musicians, as well.

In short, regardless of your level of involvement in the music business, almost anyone can fit into the definition of "musician," so if you want to learn something about the music industry, you can benefit from this book. You can be a friend, a family member of a musician, or someone who works closely with a musician. You might be a songwriter, an artist manager, a fan, or an employee of a record label or production company—essentially, a musician or any one of a number of individuals who interact with musicians in a personal or business capacity. Perhaps you aren't involved with the music industry in any way at this moment, but you are trying to gather enough information to make a decision about diving in. Even you are a musician, as far as I'm concerned. Depending on the context, throughout this book the term *"musician"* may be used interchangeably with terms such as "artist," "songwriter," or some other term describing an artist who creates and shares their skills in the music industry.

Allow me to begin by telling you what this book is *not* going to do. It's best to get this out of the way so you won't be frustrated later when you get the bad news that there's no magic formula, fairy godmother, effects pedal, pill, or contract that guarantees success in this industry. Some people sadly enter into the entertainment industry thinking fame, fortune, fans, and friends will come without having to work for it. That is simply a fantasy.

This book is not going to make you a better musician. Some musicians are under the mistaken impression that a no-talent artist who is business savvy or is surrounded by astute businesspeople somehow has a better chance at "making it" in this industry. It is important not to confuse artistic excellence with business success. Don't succumb to that temptation. Even if you are investing time in getting your business acumen together, it is crucial that you keep practicing and improving as an artist. As you will read in Chapter 5, "Artist-Management Agreements," a great business management team is valuable, but the greatest management team on earth can't keep an artist's career going if it is not backed up with some kind of identifiable, growing, and expanding talent. That part of the equation is totally up to you. Time and time again, you can see artists in every genre of entertainment that either refuse or are afraid to grow, so they repeat over and over again what made them successful. While some can sustain a career from this by having a loyal audience that wants to be reminded of "the good old days," it could be artistically disastrous for you. The best way to eliminate the possibility of suspended animation as an artist is to continue to push your creative envelope.

This book will not replace a lawyer, make you a lawyer, or eliminate legal fees. It *is* crucial for you to have a grasp of the legal workings of the music business. However, don't think that after reading this book and understanding the concepts you will be ready to handle all of the legal matters required in your career. Before trying to save the money on legal fees by handling legal matters yourself, consider the lost time and the music that you could have created during the period of time it took you to learn the art and craft of music law. You should add to that the frustration that comes with learning a skill that you might not necessarily want to learn, plus the fact that you won't do as good of a job as a trained professional. For most people who don't have the desire, attitude, or aptitude for law, handling the major legal issues that could come up in a musician's life is the equivalent of trying to do a major brake job on your car after reading a book about it. It's best to leave some things to the experts while having a clear understanding of what they are doing and why. There is no substitute for the effectiveness of a trained, experienced, and committed entertainment lawyer. This book will give you enough information to navigate the industry and discuss your legal situations more intelligently with others whom you encounter in the business, including your lawyers.

This book is not going to keep you completely up to date on the very latest trends, cases, or interpretations of the law. All you need to do is read the newspapers every day to figure out that our industry is one of the quickest moving industries in the entire world when it comes to how the law changes and how the industry is configured. Like any book trying to keep you up to date with the latest in gear technology for musicians, a book that includes the most recent legal cases would be out of date and obsolete before the ink dries. Legal and industry periodicals do a great job of keeping you informed on the latest legal issues and interpretations. Use them.

This book will not be a substitute for paying your dues. Success in the entertainment industry requires putting in a lot of time and hard work. The hoops you have to jump through, the fires you need to put out, and the artistic, financial, physical, and emotional obstacles that you face are yours and yours alone to overcome. Some people focus far too much on the legal woes of famous (and sometimes failed) artists rather than focus on what made those legal woes occur. Signing contracts without understanding them, entering into agreements with the wrong people, fearing success, acting irresponsibly, making promises that you never intended to keep, and then blaming it all on being a creative artist or businessperson who doesn't want to be bothered with such details are not legal issues—they are personal issues that all fall under the category of paying your dues as a human being and an artist. These issues cannot be sidestepped; they are all part of growing up and becoming a more responsible person. I will try to point out a few of the obstacles you may encounter in your music career and help you overcome them more easily. The information you pick up from this book could help you avoid a situation that could sidetrack your career. If so, great—then we'll both have accomplished something of significance. However, you'll still have dues to pay, so be prepared to roll up your sleeves and get to work.

Finally, this book will not in any way, shape, or form attempt to discourage you from pursuing something that is important to you. If that "something" is being a happy, creative, and well-rounded professional musician—whether for a $20 gig as a musician for one day of your life or for a 30-year career of royalties, platinum records, and a retirement plan—then by all means, give it a shot. Some books similar to this one paint such a scary picture of the entertainment industry that many musicians use them as a reason not to pursue a musical career. I mean this sincerely—if you're one of those people looking for a reason not to try, stop reading now and put this book back on the shelf. Save yourself the time. You'll eventually find your reasons to give up—if not in this book, then somewhere else. It is unrealistic and irresponsible for me to even begin to convey that everyone who wishes to carve out an artistically fulfilling and financially successful career in the entertainment industry will be able to do so. All I know is that during more than two decades in this industry, I've come across many people who have managed to make a portion of their living from the music business while maintaining some measure of sanity and happiness—enough people that I will never say it can't be done.

Enough of what reading this book won't do for you; let's take a look at what it *will* do. This book will walk you through the music industry using a relatively simplified approach. Both practicing a musical instrument and practicing law have taught me to take what appear to be very difficult challenges and break them down into workable components. I've designed this book to work the same way. It is divided into four major sections, with each section broken down further into individual components. The first section is an introduction that gives you a broad overview of the various types of legal rights that affect the music business. The second section contains overviews and explanations of the four major contracts that entertainment lawyers negotiate regularly when representing clients in the music field. The third section deals with some of the business interactions that musicians have with each other and with third parties. Part four offers a checklist of legal issues independent musicians commonly face when putting out their own product and presents a chapter on how to effectively work with a lawyer.

While the title and the point of view of this book suggest a purely legal approach to the industry, this book is intended to give you a well-rounded overview of the business. To understand the way the law works within our industry, it's important to develop an understanding of how the industry works in general. Law is never written or interpreted in a vacuum; it is usually a response or reaction to how a business evolves. The music business has evolved as a result of a combination of the development of technology, art, and society—going clear back to the printing press, up through player pianos, radio, all forms of phonograph records, and beyond to the incredible computer, telephone, and satellite technology being developed as I write this book. For example, sampling technology and the use of samples by artists in recordings led to the enforcement of copyrights affected by sampling. The enforcement of those copyrights (which included actual litigation or the threats of litigation) led to the development of standardized business practices for sampling. The resulting combination is the current practice of having to clear the use of a sample legally with the original copyright holders of both the master recording and the composition. These standards may change over time, just as many other industry standards have evolved. At the end of the day, however, it starts with the creation of a musical work and the person who created it. These are unique because every person who creates is unique. What makes the negotiation and interpretation of the law within the context of you—the creator—and the industry so interesting is that it is not static but rather ever-changing.

Another thing I set out to accomplish in this book is to introduce you to some new vocabulary, business concepts, and ways of thinking that are unique to our industry. I'm a firm believer that kindred spirits attract each other. Drummers, for example, have a unique understanding and approach to music that almost seem to spill over into a language, walk, and secret handshake that belong only to those in the "drummers club." The same goes for the business side of the music industry. With this book, I hope to demystify the legal language and concepts that often serve to confuse rather than clarify agreements between musicians and those who work with musicians. The more you can understand the language of the business, the less intimidating it will be, which will leave you more confident in making good, solid business decisions.

While it might be useful to read this book in sequence, chapter by chapter, it isn't necessary. Unless I have included a cross-reference to another chapter, you can read and use each of the chapters as a stand-alone unit. My hope is that this approach will make the book a good legal reference for years to come. For example, if you encounter an issue with your band's partnership, you can go straight to the chapter on business entities without having to read the rest of the book to gather most of the material that will apply. Of course, the information from the other chapters will help you make some decisions that may affect how you create and maintain your business entity, but for the most part, you won't have to read everything leading up to a particular chapter to understand it.

The book has been intentionally laid out with large margins to give you room to jot questions or notes into it. When I was a young French horn student, I had a teacher who encouraged me to mark up my music books because he felt is was important that I be reminded what I learned while practicing and playing the same pieces over and over. Years later, when I saw what I wrote, I could savor the artistic, emotional, and intellectual insights that had occurred. Don't be afraid of the margins—the notes that you write are probably the most important pieces of information that you will get from this book.

Each chapter will open with a short hypothetical scenario related to the general business and legal concepts covered in that chapter. Most of these hypothetical situations have been recreated as composites from actual cases that occurred in the industry at one time or another. These hypothetical situations will not cover all of the issues in the chapter; rather, they are intended to give you a quick idea of the troubles that can crop up if you don't attend to those legal issues properly. As you read each chapter, I recommend reviewing the hypothetical situation to put the theoretical and legal issues into context with the factual issues.

You will also find Companion Questions at the end of each chapter. As with the hypothetical situations, these questions are not intended to be complete checklists for your business deals; they are designed to be a starting point for the free exchange of ideas, fears, and concerns of individual parties when entering into creative and business relationships with each other. The Companion Questions are not meant to be exhaustive; once again, I encourage you to mark up the book with your answers and some questions of your own. Each deal, each person involved in the deal, and the circumstances that brought the parties together are unique and should be approached in that manner. One way to do this is to ask yourself questions that are unique to you and your deal. Taking a "companion" approach to this book, think of the Companion Questions as an experienced hiking guide asking, "Have you tried this road?" or, "What do you think will happen if you stepped on those loose rocks over there?" The questions are based on my own experiences and the number of stories—both good and bad—that I've heard from others who have traveled the path before you. Companion Questions are not intended to result in definitive directives for you to follow blindly; they are concepts and concerns for you to take into account when making your own decisions and working through your goals, actions, and deals in the business.

The most effective way to use this book is as a catalyst to learn as much as you can about the industry as a whole and each individual component of your musical career. Your goal in reading this book should be to ensure that the business relationships and the accompanying deals that you enter into throughout your career are sensible, clear, fair, and well-thought-out—commitments that you are proud to honor.

Come with me; let's take a walk together and be companions for a while.

Companion Questions

1. *What are the three most important reasons that you are involved with music?*

2. *Can you identify any people, musical groups, or companies in the music industry that you admire or want to emulate? Why do you admire them?*

3. *Have you had experiences—good or bad—or heard about others' experiences in the music industry that have affected your beliefs about what being involved in the industry is like? Are you open to altering those beliefs in any way?*

4. *Do you feel that you know how the music industry works? Are you willing to learn more?*

5. *Are you the type of person who likes to plan a trip, choosing a predetermined route and using a map while traveling, or do you like to go in a general direction, improvising your path as you go along?*

6. *If you are very well accomplished on a musical instrument, have you ever picked up a different instrument and learned how to play it without any prior instruction? If not, are you willing to do so?*

2 A Legal Primer

A phrase that I've heard and repeated a lot over the years is that "we live in a land of laws." Like it or not, just about every single part of our lives has become legislated or litigated in one way or another—from how hot coffee is served at fast-food restaurants to what constitutes indecency. It's hard to escape the effects of law on our society, and it's sometimes frustrating that it has become so entrenched in how we as citizens deal with our daily routines. Nevertheless, law has become an important component of our lives and if viewed from the right perspective can be both fascinating and fun.

In the worlds of creativity, music, entertainment, and business, the phrase "we live in a land of laws" is especially relevant. Laws have been developed and interpreted that result in how (or how not) musicians and those they deal with protect, monetize, and share their talents, personas, and creative works. This does not stop with the business side of things, either. Laws also affect how musicians as human beings and responsible citizens interact with the public and other individuals. This chapter provides a brief overview of some of the concepts behind the various laws that affect you as a musician, why these laws exist, and why they directly connect to how you wind your way through the music industry.

Hypothetical Situation: Dream or Nightmare?

A group of musicians who are longtime friends gets together every weekend, playing old rock and roll songs for the fun of it in the garage of Barry, the bass player. One day, as the musicians are warming up, they spontaneously create a song unlike any song that they have ever played before. Everyone in the band contributes to the song as it takes shape. Lyrics and melodies flow as the band members combine their musical efforts to create a great song completely from scratch. The drummer, Danny, wants to remember the great time they were all having, so he makes a visual and audio recording of their rehearsal, capturing the process of creating the entire completed original song that the band has written and performed from beginning to end.

Coincidentally, while the band is playing, a stretch limousine carrying Mr. Big, one of the biggest music executives in the country, has a flat tire in front of Barry's garage. The limo driver asks if Mr. Big can "hang out" while the tire is being fixed. The band welcomes him in, serving him lemonade as he listens. Mr. Big is impressed by their musicianship and the new song—so much, in fact, that Mr. Big calls his company and arranges for a contract to be immediately brought to the garage so Mr. Big can sign the group to a long-term exclusive artist deal. Telling them that he wants to keep the "raw, street qualities" of the band, Mr. Big asks if his company could own the song and the homemade recording to release as their first single via a variety of media including physical products of the song and recording, performances and transmissions of all types, and more. Mr. Big also asks what the name of the band is, telling them that he's never seen such rehearsal fanatics in his life. The band agrees to let him have a copy of the recording and decide on the spot that the name of the band is to be the Rehearsal Fanatics.

Six months later, the Rehearsal Fanatics are the darlings of the industry. They have sold an astonishing 4 million copies of their recording, are on a major national tour, and are appearing on late-night television shows, catapulted by the success of their unique "home movie" single and the favorable press surrounding their rags-to-riches story. Unfortunately, the fame gets to some of their heads. While leaving a concert venue, Sammy, the Fanatics' lead singer, beats up a photographer who is trying to shoot a candid photo of the band. The photographer has threatened a lawsuit against the entire band for the attack. They also find out that another band has been using the name the Rehearsal Fanatics for the past five years and is now seeking financial compensation for trademark infringement. Finally, Danny, the drummer, quits the group in the midst of all of the confusion, demanding that the rest of the group and the record label immediately stop allowing radio and television stations from using the recording that he claims that he owns. He also is making a claim against Mr. Big and the label for "stealing" his "how we made it from scratch" recording format that other acts on Mr. Big's label are now using to promote their music. The rest of the band members are now demanding to be released from their artist contract unless they get a substantial advance. The label is threatening to prevent the band from making any more records for any other label, claiming ownership of the band name.

Trouble is brewing ahead. What problems await the members of the Rehearsal Fanatics, and what bodies of law exist to settle all their potential disputes?

Personal Rights

At the core of our legal system is the recognition and protection of our personal rights as human beings. We make certain assumptions about how our daily lives are affected by each other. These assumptions are dictated largely by common sense and the fact that societies cannot function without a certain agreed-upon level of social order from its citizens to avoid chaos. All human beings have an inherent, pre-existing "zone of safety" that others shouldn't violate. For the most part, we just assume that people shouldn't harm the personal rights of other human beings.

There are certain types of unaccepted behavior in the organization of the "zone of safety" that rise to the level of criminal behavior. The elements of crimes such as murder and theft are clearly defined in the criminal codes of municipalities with the intent to keep citizens safe. Penalties are imposed by societies in forms ranging from simple warnings to incarceration or even death to enforce the criminal codes. Another level of the "zone of safety" that most societies provide to protect citizens' personal rights is conduct defined in civil codes. While not rising to the level of criminal conduct, acts such as negligently causing injury or harm to another person or their property can be the cause of action for a lawsuit brought by the harmed party against the party who harmed them in an effort to be brought whole once again.

These personal rights are at the root of the business end of the entertainment industry. Your persona—your face, name, or the image you have created in connection with the sale of any products—is protected by these personal rights. Subject to the First Amendment, for the most part, no one can use your persona without your express consent to do so. You only have to look at the fortunes made from the names and images of musicians in connection with concert tickets, commercially released recordings, and merchandise sales to understand that the rights to your persona are a very valuable asset.

On top of having your persona protected, as a musician, other important rights originate from who you are and what unique skills you develop as a person. Because of the protection of your personal rights and the fact that other people or companies cannot simply own you or your skills, what you choose to do with your unique skills and whom you share those unique skills with is ultimately up to you. If you develop your talent as a recording artist or a songwriter, you are the only person who can use your exclusive rights to your services as a recording artist or a songwriter until you give those rights away to someone else.

Property Rights

The next level of rights in our discussion consists of property rights. From the time you were a baby clutching a stuffed animal and screaming "MINE!" to checking the accuracy of your seven-figure royalty check for a hit recording, you probably have a sense of what property rights are and how valuable they can be. There are three major legal categories of property: *Real Property* (e.g., real estate, homes, and water rights), *Personal Property* (e.g., all forms of money, cars, and musical instruments), and *Intellectual Property* (e.g., copyrights, trademarks, and patents). Without discounting the importance of your understanding of the nature and extreme value of Real Property or Personal Property and how these types of property fit into the rights that affect what you do or earn as a musician, the major focus of this property rights overview in the music industry is on your creative assets—your Intellectual Property.

Intellectual Property is self-defining: It is the property of the intellect, the property of the mind. You can't feel or touch intellectual property initially, because it lives in your brain, waiting to come out in a flash of brilliance through some tangible form, such as the name of your band, a song, or a killer guitar riff that you record. One of the intentions of the United States Constitution was to encourage citizens to use their minds to create. As our nation advanced and continues to do so through the tools of technology, these various forms of creation have become "monetized" or converted into financial reward as laws offered the creators different kinds of protections for the different kinds of intellectual property that they produced. These laws eventually developed into the whole field of intellectual property that we have today.

Let's look at some examples of intellectual property, how it is protected, and how you, as the owner of that property, can use that protection to convert intellectual property into something of value that can be traded in commerce.

Inventions are a form of intellectual property protected by patents. While this is a highly complex and technical field well beyond the scope of this brief overview, in basic terms, when you create a new invention or a process for doing something, it could warrant applying for a patent to protect it. If the Patent and Trademark Office determines that your invention or process is original and issues you a patent, that patent would give you the exclusive right to exploit your invention for a set period of time. During this period of exclusivity, others who would like to create and sell products using your patent would have to pay you a negotiated fee to use your patent. Examples of patents in the music industry over the years include equipment inventions (e.g., the electric guitar), new processes (e.g., methods of sound production in synthesizers), and improvements in technology (e.g., the shape, design, and materials used for guitar cable tips).

Another form of intellectual property is a trade secret. If you were to come up with an idea that is original, identifiable, and unique, a possible way to protect it would be to enter into a non-disclosure agreement (NDA) with anyone to whom you may disclose your idea. Given the great advances in technology that have resulted in the relatively inexpensive yet incredibly fast pace at which ideas can be turned into products, the NDA is a very important and highly effective document. For example, if you were to develop a concept for a music-based audiovisual show that could be produced and then transmitted in multiple media formats (e.g., radio, television, telephone, and computer transmissions), your concept could potentially be an extremely valuable secret. The NDA is the formal legal equivalent of putting your index finger across your lips, lowering your voice to a whisper, and saying, "Shhh ... don't tell anyone this secret or use it without my permission." If the people to whom you disclosed your idea should use that idea, you could seek damages from them for your loss of potential revenue and business due to the breach of your non-disclosure agreement. However, if people to whom you are disclosing your idea had independent previous knowledge of your idea (they may have worked on a similar kind of project or product in the past) or if your idea is not unique and is relatively common knowledge to the general public, it would be difficult for you to enforce an NDA.

Unique skills are another kind of intellectual property often protected by agreement in the music industry. This is a variation of the spirit of the NDA and is called a non-competition agreement. When businesses pay huge amounts of money to individuals because of their unique artistic or executive talents, they want to know that the purchase of those unique talents will not be available to competitors. For example, when one record company purchases another, it is not unusual for the purchasing company to ask the departing executives of the purchased company to refrain from running another label for a reasonable period of time. This gives the purchasing company time to establish itself in the marketplace without fear of the competition that made the purchased company valuable in the first place. Most courts try not to prevent people from making a living, however, so the courts closely consider the length, geographical area, and scope of non-competition agreements to make sure that they are fair and reasonable.

Patents, trade secrets, and unique services are all valuable and important types of intellectual property that are protected regularly in our industry. However, the importance of their protection does not compare to the prevalence and importance of what I like to refer to as the "big two" forms of intellectual property in our industry: trademarks and copyrights.

Trademark and Copyright

You don't have to look very hard to see that trademarks in the music industry surround us. Names of acts, record labels, slogans, names of tours, and brands of musical instruments are all examples of marks that are valuable commodities in the entertainment business. Making a distinctive trade name identifiable to the public can be the difference between success and failure for any kind of business venture. This becomes especially crucial in our industry, where brand recognition and loyalty are the keys to making sure that audiences keep coming back to buy tickets, recordings, and other products.

The intellectual property protected by trademark law is the source of goods or services. Trademarks are the names used in connection with goods; service marks are the names used in connection with services. For simplicity, I will refer to both of them as trademarks. By creating, maintaining, and protecting a strong trademark, your business can exclusively use the trademark and prevent others from using it. Because only you own and can legally use the trademark, it helps prevent confusion in the marketplace as to the source of the goods bearing that mark. Exclusive rights to use trademarks are sought by businesses such as bands or record labels because the owners want their business to have an identity distinct from all the other businesses in the same field.

To establish a trademark, you must first make sure that your trademark is a fanciful name, not one that is simply descriptive. For example, "The Purple Iodine Twins" is more likely to be considered a valid trademark than "A Band with Two Guitarists and a Singer." One way to establish your trademark in the marketplace is simply by using it. For example, if you are an act, using your name on promotional materials and recordings is an excellent way to introduce your trademark in the marketplace. The strength and extent of your trademark in the marketplace is determined through your consistent usage of the trademark over time. If you live in a small town on the East Coast of the United States, and only play live shows that are limited to within the borders of your town, it would be difficult to prevent another band on the other side of the country from using the same name. However, if you have musical products like CDs or digital downloads available to the entire nation through a website, your marketplace is extended accordingly.

You can also take steps to legally secure a trademark before actually using it by applying for trademark registration through the U.S. Patent and Trademark Office under an "intent to use" status. When using this method, you can essentially reserve the right to a trademark until you are ready to use it in the marketplace. A great deal of helpful information can be found at the United States Patent and Trademark Office website, www.uspto.gov.

Distinct from all of the other types of intellectual property, copyright law protects the expression of an idea in a tangible medium. Obviously, this spreads far and wide as copyright law includes the protection of musical compositions, audio and visual recordings, photographs, artwork, lyrics, and computer programs. Two important and distinct protections of copyright in connection with music stand out above the rest and need to be clearly understood throughout this book and beyond. The creation, protection, and exploitation of musical compositions (songs) are protected by the Performing Arts (PA) copyright that is the basis of the music publishing business. Hand in hand with the protection of songs, the creation, protection, and exploitation of master recordings (all configurations of "records," including vinyl recordings played on turntables, CDs, and digital downloads) are protected by the Sound Recording (SR) copyrights that make up what we've come to know as the recording or record business. The combination of these two versions of copyrights is the basis of virtually the entire music economic landscape.

Copyright ownership is established as soon as the expression of an idea is fixed in a tangible medium. An idea alone (e.g., the concept of love or world peace) is not protected by copyright. If you wrote your expression of love or world peace, it does not give you the right to stop anyone else from writing their own expression of those same ideas. The tangible medium can take a variety of forms—anything from writing lyrics on a piece of scrap paper to recording a song on your computer to making a full-blown studio recording with an entire band. The creation of the copyrighted work is not to be confused with the registration of the work with the Register of Copyrights at the Library of Congress. Think of copyright registration as having a record of your work in a centralized database that provides a much more convenient way to prove your ownership than searching through your own files. The copyright law encourages you to register your works by providing for added benefits in the event of copyright infringement of your registered work. These benefits include the possible awarding of statutory money damages and attorneys' fees in the case of infringement.

Once a song or master recording is created, a number of rights are attached to it. These rights include the exclusive right of the copyright holder to make copies, to perform, to display, to make changes, and to publish sound recordings by way of digital transmission, and to make phonorecordings of all configurations of the work. The ability to make and sell recordings, to collect money from radio or public performances, and to use the recordings or songs on television or movies is based on the rights established by copyright. Details of how you deal with others in your protection and business dealings in connection with these rights will be discussed more fully in Chapters 3 and 4 in connection with songwriter agreements and artist agreements.

Copyright infringement—also known as plagiarism—requires two elements. One is that the infringing work needs to sound substantially similar to the original. The second is that the infringing party must have had access to the original work.

The subject of copyright infringement is a good opportunity to point out an industry practice that many novices find quite frustrating: the rejection of unsolicited demo submissions. In an effort to avoid potential copyright infringement actions, many music industry businesses simply do away with the second element of the infringement equation by not accepting submissions unless the person submitting it has a preexisting connection to the business. The logic is pretty straightforward:

If no one associated with the business ever heard the work, no one at the company could have copied it. This practice can be very frustrating to anyone without an "in," who might logically interpret the industry as being one of exclusion and "old boy" networking. I will not deny that such networking is a reality in any social and business situation. I will also encourage those who are frustrated by this apparent exclusion to keep trying, because eventually they will find a way through the door. Just remember that it's usually a lawyer's opinion keeping your submission from getting through the door, not the hard-working creative people listening to the music.

Intellectual property law is exciting and challenging because it is always fueled by technology. From the printing press to the lightning-fast personal computers of today, the technology that affects the music business changes almost daily, making intellectual property law one of the most fluid bodies of law ever. For these reasons, while I intend to keep up to date, I will approach intellectual property law throughout this book in broad strokes and general terms, especially as it relates to the ever-changing issues of music distribution via developing technology such as computers, cell phones, satellite technology, the Internet, and whatever other forms the incredible human brain can think of.

Contract Rights

The issues surrounding personal and property rights should not encourage musicians to function forever alone in a vacuum. We live in a society that encourages human interaction, especially when it comes to creating and sharing music. Those who interact with each other need to establish boundaries, ground rules, and consequences for breaking the rules. The resulting body of law is contract law, the law that governs and protects agreements between people. Many entertainment lawyers spend their entire careers negotiating and drafting the various agreements that are special to our industry. The second section of this book is devoted to helping you understand the various roles of the parties of these contracts, their respective desires, the background of the development of these contracts, the elements involved, and some of the subtleties of these specialized contracts. It has been my experience that armed with a clear knowledge of what "the other side" expects in contractual relationships, parties to agreements enter into them with much less suspicion and trepidation.

Specialties

Other law specialties come into play as you grow as an artist and business. For example, if you are touring internationally, immigration law is important. Corporate and employment law are crucial as your team and business grow. At some point in your career, you may encounter situations that will require seeking further legal knowledge and/or advice on taxes, family and marital matters, criminal issues, and First Amendment issues. These specialties and variations will be discussed in detail in Chapter 12.

In summary, the law dealing with your personal rights, property rights, and contractual relationships form the foundation of what you need to know to understand many of the facets of the music business. Using this brief overview and introduction of the law as a backdrop, we can proceed with greater detail toward an even better understanding of "the machine."

Companion Questions

1. *Are you a proactive personality or a reactive personality?*

2. *Do you proceed with caution and sure footing, or are you a risk taker?*

3. *Do you feel that paperwork and formalities slow down or inhibit the creative process?*

4. *When developing personal and business relationships of any kind, do you carefully screen the people with whom you get involved or do you enter into your relationships quickly and sort out the details as you go along?*

5. *What are the various types of intellectual property that you can or intend to create? Do you understand or are you willing to learn how to protect these properties?*

6. *As you grow as a musician, is there a specific persona you are trying to create, develop, and convey to the industry and to the public?*

7. *Reflecting on how you have answered the preceding questions, would you rather document your creative path with a contract law, "front-end" negotiation approach or wait for issues to arise and then take care of them with a dispute-resolution, "back-end" negotiation approach?*

8. *Do you enjoy the business dealings of the music business?*

The Four Agreements

3 Songwriting and Music Publishing Agreements

I cannot write the following phrase enough times, and feel it from the bottom of my heart every single time I do so: *It starts with a song.* Period. There is absolutely no music business without the music. This entire industry would be nothing if it weren't for songwriters and their songs.

Think about it for a moment—when trying to remember a particular time in your life, what do you use as an artistic reference point? It's usually by identifying the songs you were listening to or singing at the time. Even more to the point in the context of the music industry, have you ever asked yourself what was more important—an act or a song? I personally believe that it's the song, because if you are trying to identify an act, you usually do so by referring to the songs that they performed. Long after an act has vanished from public view and popularity, the act's songs seem carry on in the form of radio play, soundtracks, and remakes or cover versions performed by other acts.

Whether these songs are created by craftsmen and -women who toiled for enormous lengths of time to develop their skills, pay their dues, and deliver angst-driven, passionate expressions of their inner most feelings, or through cute, spontaneous sparks of inspiration somehow stumbled upon by people of little or no musical talent, the result is still the same. Someone captured lightning in a bottle and that lightning came out as an expression of art in the form of music. If you are a composer who writes music, a lyricist who writes the words that go with music, or some combination of the two, you can go to sleep every night knowing that the result of your work—the music—is the foundation of the music industry.

Because of the importance of songs, one of the most valuable assets of any music-based company is the copyright of musical works. The controversies surrounding the ownership and business control of some of the most revered collections of copyrights in musical history are legendary. Tracing the ownership of the Beatles' songs, the Motown hits of the 1960s, and the songs of masters such as George Gershwin is the musical equivalent of an archeological dig into the history of our industry. The song catalogs of the great songwriters and the popular artists of our time are treated like the crown jewels for good reason: These songs can be worth literally millions of dollars. This all matters to you because when it comes to compiling a publishing catalog, the very first transaction made in the chain of ownership is the agreement between the publishing company that owns the song and the person who originally wrote it. This agreement is the songwriter-publisher agreement. If you are a songwriter, signing even just one of these agreements could be the single most important moment in your career. Some background information will help you better understand the impact of a songwriter-publisher agreement.

As stated in Chapter 2, there are two primary copyrights that affect musicians: the Performing Arts (PA) copyright and the Sound Recording (SR) copyright. The music publishing business, which this chapter of *The Musician's Legal Companion* focuses on, concerns the songs themselves (the PA copyright), whereas the record business deals with the masters on which those songs are recorded (the SR copyright). Chapter 4 covers the SR copyright and other aspects of the record business. While closely tied to each other, these two facets of the industry are clearly distinguishable, so you should learn the details of them separately and keep them separated like apples and oranges in your industry business dealings, just as the major music corporations do.

Hypothetical Situation: Songwriting
Wendy regularly collaborates with Connie. The two of them split all costs of making their demo recordings. They divide all aspects of their collaboration evenly, including creative ideas, ownership, writing credits, and any business decisions about their songs. Each retains separate ownership and control of her respective shares of the co-written songs. This gives them the freedom to seek separate publishing deals with different publishing companies if they so choose.

Wendy plays in a band signed to an independent label that has major label distribution. This band has other members who write, too, and Wendy often collaborates with those writers. Together, Wendy and Connie have published more than 20 of their co-written songs that have either been recorded by Wendy's band or used on television shows, in movies, or recorded on independent projects by other artists.

Wendy and Connie share a healthy hobby, as well. They are both basketball fanatics who play in pick-up games every Saturday afternoon. One of the ways that they "test drive" their songs is to record demos of their original material, compile their demos with popular songs of the day, and then play this compilation loudly during their basketball games to see how the players react to their songs. One particular Saturday, one of their songs, "I'm Driving to My Goal," caused the basketball game to come to a complete halt. Each of the players commented on how inspiring and professional the song was. After letting their teammates know that they wrote the song, Wendy and Connie were inundated with praise and awe. They soaked in the admiration of their fellow athletes as they continued their games for the day.

Later, when the pick-up game had broken up for the day, Ivan, one of the basketball players, sheepishly approached Wendy and Connie. Ivan told them that even though he wasn't a songwriter or musician, he wanted to let them know that he really liked their song but thought it was missing something. He explained in his non-musical way what his thoughts were. After some discussion, the two collaborators concluded that Ivan was absolutely right. Using Ivan's idea, they added a bridge to the song. The revision in the song improved it dramatically, so Wendy and Connie enthusiastically brought their reworked version of the song to their next pick-up game. They let Ivan hear it, asked for his approval (which he gladly gave them), and then promised to make him an even collaborator in the song. They filled out a copyright registration form, naming Ivan as one of the three songwriters, and gave him a copy of the form along with a letter signed by all three of them confirming the equal splits to the song. A few weeks later, Ivan dropped out of the pick-up game, never to be seen again. The only permanent address that Wendy and Connie had for Ivan was his mother's home address.

Connie and Wendy included the three-way collaboration when they sent out their next round of demos to their music industry contacts several months later. While waiting for responses to their song-writing demos, the music publishing division of the large conglomerate distributing Wendy's band's music made a policy decision that all artist/writers who were signed to distributed labels were required to sign music publishing agreements to the company, as well. The lawyers for the publishing company were instructed to attempt to obtain the rights for all songs written prior to the execution of any agreement, provided the rights were still available.

Out of the blue, Connie got a phone call from a big-time record producer whom she met at a party. The producer wanted a very famous major label artist to record "I'm Driving To My Goal" for the sound track for a major motion picture about a pick-up basketball player who makes it to the pro ranks. The producer excitedly told Connie that the song was being considered as the "big radio single" to be used as the theme song to carry the entire soundtrack recording in the cross-promotion of the movie. There was also talk about immediately turning the movie into a television series, with "I'm Driving To My Goal" as the theme song for the first season. All the producer and the movie's music supervisor need to move forward is the "green light" from all three publishers of the song to start recording. They also need an idea of how much money they all want as a synchronization fee to put it in the movie. The major label artist being considered to record "I'm Driving to My Goal" also wants to know if he can make some "minor changes" in the song to make it fit his style. If he makes these stylistic changes, he wants to know what percentage ownership of the song he will receive for his work.

What do Wendy, Connie, and Ivan do now?

Creative Considerations

Before looking at some of the legal aspects associated with music publishers and the music publishing industry, the first tier of legal issues that arises has to do with the creation of the musical work itself. How is it created? Who created it? When was it created? How can I change it? Who owns the music and, if we share ownership, how do we share ownership? While these legal thoughts are likely to be far from your brain, heart, and soul when you are caught up in the moment of creating something as emotional and passionate as a song, all of them are potential landmines that need to be deftly danced around when you consider the consequences of ignoring them.

As briefly stated in Chapter 2, a work is protected by copyright when fixed in a tangible medium. This means that it is reduced to a recorded form that is no longer simply "floating" in space. When working alone, this process can be pretty straightforward. Inspiration hits, you mull it around for as long as you like, perhaps perform it a few times to test drive the song and hear what is sounds like, revise and edit it in your head, and then eventually, fix it in some tangible form. This fixing process can be anything from putting pen to paper, recording it with an audio or video recorder, or entering data into a computer.

Collaboration

The "gestation period" of a song's development prior to putting it in tangible form sometimes comes into question when working with other people, because it brings into question whether or not the actual composition was completed before anyone else touched it, as well as what elements were attributable to which parties. These questions of creation and collaboration often are issues of contention for those who write together. Before charging forward with these issues, I would like to review two elements that are not protected by copyright. One is the *idea* of the song, the other is the *title* of the song. So, if you bring a song about baseball to your band titled "Bring Them All Home" and let them rehearse it, you cannot stop anyone in the band from creating their own expression in the form of a song about the subject of baseball, and you cannot stop them from using the title "Bring Them All Home," regardless of what the song is about.

I highly recommend that if you are going to let others listen to your musical composition with even the slightest intention of collaborating with them in a clear, identifiable direction, it is a good idea to make a simple recording for them to listen to. This way, you have established the work in a fixed and tangible medium, so it is protected, and it gives you a clear, objective "starting point" to work from to determine if any additional creative input from potential collaborators should be characterized as collaborating (also referred to as co-writing), or if the input is simply arrangement, production, or incidental enhancement of a completed song.

Be aware that these are artistic and creative decisions, so in many cases they are subjective determinations that aren't very cut and dry—particularly when such things as musical genre are taken into account. For example, in dance, R&B, rock, and hip-hop songs, rhythm patterns and the specific elements associated with those rhythm patterns—no matter how simple they may be—can be the most important and memorable parts of the song. In these cases, the grooves essentially become the song itself rather than a supporting background element to a pre-existing song. The same goes for a distinctive guitar or keyboard riff that becomes part of the essence of a song.

It's a good idea to have a clear understanding with potential collaborators about how a collaborative songwriting session will be run, and what the potential results of your collaborative work will be. Despite the most detailed formalities, intentions, and preparation with your songwriting, often the very best and most inspired works come from the spontaneous jamming, grooving, and a shared feeling that comes when minds, hearts, instruments, and music meet in the moment. If this results in music that can eventually be fixed in a tangible medium, be sure to take the time to have an open, sharing, creative, and business-based discussion about the fruits of your labor and creativity.

Sometimes collaborators formalize the details regarding their collaborative works into a collaboration contract, which incorporates the various elements of the collaboration into a document that can be referred to if there are any questions at all about a song. Some key elements of your collaboration discussion will be to determine who was responsible for what elements of the composition; what (if any) material changes you are willing to let each other make in the composition; what the percentage ownership shares of the song will be; if one person will be designated as the spokesperson for all business dealings in connection with the song, or if all collaborators will contribute; and who signs documents in connection with uses of the song.

Probably the most argued and varied discussion of collaboration agreements—formal or not—is the percentage split between the writers of a song. Some writers devise relatively elaborate formulas for determining these amounts based on factors such as time spent writing, whether or not music or lyrics are more important, and the actual number of words in the song, among other factors. Others take a more organic approach and split their songwriting evenly regardless of the input of the parties writing. You can come up with your own way of determining these figures; just remember that these splits are a negotiated percentage and it is best to negotiate these splits sooner than later. Creative minds are much more civil, clear, objective, and rational when making these decisions well before tens of thousands of dollars in royalties are waiting in the wings to be disbursed by a record label. Note that on a copyright registration form there is no blank space to write in what the percentage splits are. This means that the presumption (at least from looking at the official record of the copyright registration form) is that the collaborators are splitting their shares equally.

Without a specific grant of administration rights from collaborators to a fellow collaborator or other designated publisher, agent, or representative of some kind, the collaborators all retain their respective rights to grant licenses and permissions to third parties as long as they keep each other informed about any such licenses and account to each other for monies earned from them. One particular license, however, concerns the first time a song is recorded. If you were the co-writer of a song, you and your collaborators may have to evaluate if you would collectively benefit more by trying to have an established artist record it instead of you recording and releasing it yourself—particularly if you don't have the same wide audience and promotions push as an established artist. Copyright holders must agree on the issuance of the initial mechanical license granted to allow a song to be recorded and introduced to the public as a phonorecord. Subsequent to the release of that recording to the public through sales and distribution (but not for demonstration purposes), anyone can record the song subject to notifying and paying the then-current statutory royalties to the respective copyright holders through the compulsory mechanical license provisions of the copyright act. Mechanical licenses are discussed in further detail below, as well as in Chapter 10.

Work For Hire

Sometimes writers are hired by someone else to write musical compositions with the intent that the hiring party will be the owner and copyright holder in the composition. This is what is known as a *work-for-hire* arrangement, which is essentially a contract for a composer to produce a commissioned work. In the work-for-hire arrangement, the party commissioning the piece of music becomes the author of the work; the person delivering the music is simply providing a technical service. For example, if an advertising agency were to give you all of the guidelines for a piece of music, let you use its studio to record it, and control the creative aspects of the work, the advertising agency would be considered the creator and copyright owner of the work, and your services would be considered as a work for hire. When providing music for someone as a work for hire, it is good practice to have a written contract that sets out the specific scope of the project for which you are writing, the price you are being paid, and whether you are to receive further payments or other compensation for uses of the work outside of the scope of what you were hired to do.

Sources of Income

Now that we've looked at the creation of the music works, what can be done with them once you have them in hand? Copyrights of musical compositions generate money from five major sources: mechanical income, performance income, synchronization income, print income, and new media income. Together, these sources of income are the bread and butter of songwriters who devote their entire careers to crafting songs, as well as those who have stumbled upon a hit by pure luck.

Historically, the easiest source of income to identify has been mechanical income. Owners of copyrights to songs issue licenses *(mechanical licenses)* to manufacturers of media products that require a mechanical device to play the songs. The mechanical devices used to play music historically have included player pianos, 8-track tape players, phonographs, cassette decks, portable CD players, and as of this writing, hand-held devices and telephones that play digitally downloaded recordings of music. The technology has changed—and will continue to—over time, but the basic concept of a mechanical license remains: If a mechanical device is required to hear the music, the party that manufactures and distributes the recordings is required to obtain a license from the owner of the copyright of the musical compositions embodied on the recordings in order to make those recordings. A means for establishing the license fee for a mechanical license was included in the 1976 Copyright Law and has been referred to as the "statutory rate" for a license. This rate has varied over time, rising from slightly around 2 cents to more than 9 cents per unit manufactured and sold. Since the eventual license fee is a royalty based on units sold, it is clear that the more units sold, the more money is generated for the writers of the compositions. The Harry Fox Agency is a company that has represented a great number of publishers with respect to the issuance and administration of mechanical licenses. While you need to decide independently if you want to utilize the services of the Harry Fox Agency or any other licensing agency to handle your licensing matter, I highly recommend visiting their website at www.harryfox.com for a thorough discussion of mechanical licenses and the most up-to-date statutory rates.

Notwithstanding the existence of statutory rates and compulsory rates, it is still possible for parties to negotiate rates for mechanical licenses. For example, a record label that is producing recordings of a composition can contact a publisher and negotiate a discounted rate (e.g., 75 percent of the then-current statutory rate) instead of the full rate for recordings manufactured and sold.

Some quick math will illustrate the importance of mechanical royalties to a songwriter's career. If a long-playing recording including 10 songs at a rate of 9.1 cents earns Recording Industry Association of America (RIAA) gold record status (500,000 units sold), it would generate more than $450,000 in mechanical royalties alone. When you think of the songwriters that are in the relative background supplying songs to multiplatinum-selling recording artists who spend more time in the public eye, consider which of those two career paths you would rather pursue.

The second source of income from the use of songs is performance income. Performance rights for musical compositions are separated into two categories. The first category is *grand performance rights,* which covers uses of music on stage in connection with performances such as operas, plays, or dance performances in a dramatic setting where there is narration, a plot, and/or costumes and scenery. Uses other than grand performance rights usually fall into the category of *small performance rights.* Common examples of small performance rights include performances of songs on traditional so-called "terrestrial" radio, satellite radio, and television, as well as Internet streaming, telephone on-hold services, and in retail stores, bars, clubs, and concerts, among other uses.

One of the major differences between grand and small performance rights is how use licenses are negotiated and paid. Grand performance licenses are negotiated directly between the user of the music and the music publisher. If, for example, a producer of a musical were negotiating a grand performance license, negotiating a fee would include points such as the amount of music being used, how long the anticipated run would be, and whether the musical was to go on tour.

Small performance rights, on the other hand, are negotiated, granted, administered, and paid out to songwriters and publishers in the United States by the three performance rights organizations, ASCAP, BMI, and SESAC. Songwriters and music publishers affiliate with one of these performance rights organizations (PROs) and grant the PRO the right to represent their interests in the administration and collection of small performance rights royalties. The PRO negotiates and grants *blanket licenses* to end users (such as radio stations) for the right to use all of the music represented by the PRO. The fees for these blanket licenses vary widely based on a variety of factors. For example, when determining a radio station's fee, facts such as signal strength, location, and popularity are considered; a license for a gym would factor in square footage, number of exercise classes using music, and number of members. Through an elaborate combination of statistical analysis, accounting, and survey methodolgies that track the music that is used by the end users, the PRO calculates which songs are played and how much each songwriter and publisher should be paid from the fees negotiated with end users. It is not unusual for a song that is a multiformat hit on the radio (for example, a song that is both an R&B and pop hit) and used on television to generate hundreds of thousands of dollars in small performance royalties over time. Choosing a PRO to represent you is one of the more important decisions you can make in the industry, so research them well before making your choice.

A third major source of income for songwriters is *synchronization,* or *sync,* fees, which are the fees paid for the use of songs in synchronization with videos, film, and television. With the explosion of television programming due to the expansion of cable television stations and the cross-promotion of recorded music and movies, sync income has become a significant source of income for songwriters and publishers. Negotiation for the dollar amount of sync licenses varies widely; factors include whether a song was a hit, how much of the song is being used, how the song is being used, and how much of the production budget is set aside for music licenses. It is not out of the ordinary for a major motion picture to spend tens of thousands of dollars to use a hit song if the song is important to the movie. Sync income also becomes quite lucrative when a song is tied in to a product for advertising purposes. Companies will pay upwards of hundreds of thousands of dollars—sometimes even millions of dollars—for the use of songs in major multiyear advertising campaigns.

In the infancy of the music industry, print income was the major source of income for songwriters and publishers. Print income is a great example of how technology has affected the music publishing industry in a big way. In the early 1900s, radio and phonographs were not yet commonplace, so the primary method of sharing music was through the sale of sheet music. All you needed was someone in your household who played a musical instrument and could read music. Songs made popular through live performances became sheet music hits, generating most of the income for songwriters and their publishers. With the development of technology, the sales of printed music became a smaller proportion of the money generated by music. Today, the online sharing of chord charts and tablature by musicians has diminished the popular sheet music trade significantly. Nevertheless, there will always be a market for printed music in the form of "best of" books, folios, arrangements, and fake books.

Finally, we have the evolving arena of "new media" income. This source of income is somewhat mislabeled because, as with established forms of technology (such as radio and audiotape), what is new today will be superceded in the immediate and distant future. From peer-to-peer file sharing to what is considered a mechanical device, the standards for these new uses are being negotiated, renegotiated, and formulated in real time as the technology industry, the music industry, and the music-buying public work together to find a way to keep the "music dollar" flowing through to those who create the music. Developing these standards requires striking a delicate balance between a musician's and a music company's right to be paid for their work and the need to deliver music to the public in a way that satisfies the music buyer and keeps up with the times.

Based on these sources of income, the music publishing business developed. The job of the music publisher is to find talented writers, obtain the copyrights to the writer's songs, find as many uses for the songs as possible, and handle the administrative tasks in connection with the licensing, collection, and distribution of income generated from the songs. With the emergence of artists who write their own material and independent producers who create a demand for their production services by writing songs that artists want to record, the music publishing business has merged closer than ever with the record side of the business. Publishing companies no longer simply look for writers, they look for writers who might have a good chance of making it as a recording artist or a producer. By signing an act or a producer to a publishing deal, the chances of having multiple songs hit the marketplace are greatly increased.

The Writer-Publisher Agreement

With these creative and business considerations as a backdrop, the relationship of songwriter and publisher is formed. On one hand, you have a songwriter who owns the copyrights to his or her songs;

on the other is the music publisher who has the contacts, experience, and desire to obtain the greatest amount of exposure and income from the same songs. The most basic and traditional contractual arrangement between the two parties is one in which the writer sells all the ownership of her songs to the publisher in exchange for a royalty earned from the use of the songs. The generally accepted songwriter royalty is 50 percent of the income earned from the exploitation of the song—the so-called Traditional Publishing Deal. While everything and anything is negotiable in our industry, I rarely see less than a 50 percent royalty paid to a writer in a songwriter-publisher deal. Beyond the basic split of royalties, a variety of major negotiation points arise in the songwriter–publisher relationship.

What Is Included in the Catalog?

At the outset, a songwriter and publisher need to determine which songs to include in their publishing agreement. They can determine this in a variety of ways. First of all, the agreement could be song-based; such an agreement is typically referred to as a *single song* agreement even though it could comprise more than one song. Imagine playing a demo of 50 of your songs for a publisher who then chooses only 15 specific songs that she's excited about. The agreement would specifically refer to only those copyrights identified by the two of you to be included in your relationship. Absent any kind of option or restriction by the publisher to pick up the rest of your catalog, you are free to make single-song deals with any other publisher for the balance of your songs.

A slight variation of the single-song agreement is one that is based on a triggering event such as the release of a recording. Say, for example, a record label wants to enter into a publishing agreement with you that includes the songs that are released by the label. At the time you enter into the publishing agreement, the songs that are subject to the agreement might not have been picked for the project yet; chances are that you haven't even written the songs yet. However, when the project is finally released, the particular copyrights subject to the publishing agreement can be identified and incorporated into the agreement as in a single-song deal.

The most traditional version of the writer-publisher agreement is called a *term agreement,* in which all of the compositions that you write during a certain term determine the extent of the catalog owned by the publisher. The term agreement sets a period of time during which you, as a writer, are providing your services exclusively for the publisher. Most term agreements establish a minimum number of songs that must be submitted during the period.

The length of a term deal is a major negotiation point. Publishing contracts are usually set for an initial period such as a calendar year, and the publisher can exercise a series of options to extend the contract for subsequent similar periods of time. I've seen negotiated exclusive terms go from as short as two years to as long as seven; it's all negotiable. On the writer's side, there is a desire to have as much freedom as possible to move around as a free agent. On the publisher's side, there's the desire to be able to create a demand for the writer and to capitalize on the mutual success as long as possible. Both arguments are valid in my book and should be carefully thought through by all parties.

Who Owns What?

As discussed earlier, the ownership of property is the most important issue of any agreement throughout the entertainment industry, and music publishing is no exception. Amassing a catalog of songs is the primary goal of a publisher, so don't be surprised when you are asked to sell anywhere from 50 to 100 percent of the copyright ownership of your songs to the publisher. The writer, will, of course, retain 100 percent ownership of the so-called "writer portion" of the song. At this juncture, I often have heard songwriters express a great deal of hesitance over the years. "But these songs are *mine!* They mean so much to me ... I just can't let anyone else own even a part of them!" If this is truly the case, then perhaps ultimately self-ownership should win out over financial, emotional, and physical health issues. However, unless you as a writer have the means, desire, connections, and wherewithal to publish the songs yourself, accept the reality that you may own a private collection: a catalog of songs that will not be heard by the public at large but only by the people you hand-pick to hear them.

Conversely, if you do have the ability to get your songs heard and placed, why sell them to someone else? For example, if you produce other artists, if you or an associate has the ability to place your songs with recording projects or sync opportunities, or if you are an artist who is experiencing a certain amount of success by recording and performing your own songs, you might not need to enter into a publishing agreement at all if the publisher requires ownership of your songs. Keep them; in this case, your "private collection" isn't so private after all.

Administration Rights

Whether or not the publisher owns all or part of your songs, it is likely that she would want to obtain 100 percent of the *administration rights* to the songs. Administration rights are wholly distinct and separate from copyright ownership rights; they are the rights to deal with the songs in the normal course of the music publishing business. It would be cumbersome for the publisher to have to ask you (and all of the other songwriters whose songs are owned or administered by the publisher) for your permission or signature every time she wants to do anything with your songs. The administration rights give publishers the freedom to send out demos to seek uses, license the songs to others, collect royalties generated from the songs, handle the paperwork necessary to register the copyright in the songs, and perform similar tasks.

Songwriting Commitment

Ask yourself this question: "If I were writing full-time, how many songs could I write in a day? A week? A month? A year?" That's the very question that a publisher asks when you enter into an exclusive writing agreement. Publishing agreements usually look for a minimum level of productivity from writers, requiring a commitment of a certain number of songs during each term. Pay close attention to how the agreement defines your minimum commitment. Some publishing agreements count any songs that are completed in some sort of demo recording form during the term; others count only songs that are recorded and released by major label artists or used in major studio motion pictures or network television shows. Additionally, minimum commitments only count your proportional part of a co-written song.

Depending on which of these definitions your agreement adopts, a 10-song minimum commitment could mean 10 demos turned in by a solo writer, or it could mean one writer with two collaborators delivering 30 songs that are commercially released on audio recordings or used on network broadcast television shows. Clearly, these are two completely different degrees of difficulty when it comes to delivery by the two writers.

As with many agreements in the entertainment industry, commitment terms are negotiable. A songwriter who writes full-time and hopes to have other artists perform his or her songs will enter into a different agreement than a band that cowrites and puts out an album every year or two. Before settling on a commitment number, factor in as many things as possible to determine if you are being realistic about how much you can deliver. For example, think about how much you collaborate with others, how quickly you write, if you sample songs (which might diminish your proportional share of songs), and what your other professional commitments are (if you are also an artist who has to record, tour, and promote a release, you probably have less time on your hands than a writer who isn't a recording artist). If you fail to meet the minimum commitment, your contract can be suspended, which extends the length of the contract until the minimum is met.

Advances and Recoupments

Monetary advances are always a lively point of discussion when evaluating and negotiating any kind of agreement between an artist and another party. Many times, it becomes a substantial and central focus of discussion that eclipses every other important point in the agreement. Don't let it. While money is important—sometimes crucial—it is not the absolute be all and end all of your deal. Chapter 8, "Other People's Money," discusses this even further, but for now, let's look at what affects the likelihood, value, and effect of advances on your publishing deal.

First of all, let's agree on the definition. An *advance* is money that the publisher pays up front and expects to see later. Your advance is tied in to the publisher's timing of payment to you and the eventual return of that payment. In most cases, music business companies—publishers included—will not advance money to writers unless there is a strong and calculated belief that the writer's songs can and will generate sufficient royalties to pay back the advance. Although there are exceptions to this rule, for the most part the publisher is not gambling, but instead making a solid investment based on information that you provide.

Publishers sometimes advance certain costs in connection with their business. These costs can include demo costs (studio rental, musician fees, vocalist fees, and so on), equipment or materials costs, duplication costs, and other expenses. Depending on your situation, a publisher may also advance costs for you to travel for songwriting seminars, networking opportunities, and other promotional costs. The underlying spirit here is that the publisher is more likely to spend money if it is beneficial to both of you.

Of course, there is also the writer advance, which goes right into your pocket. You can do a few things to make the publisher more likely to pay out a writer advance. One of them is to have money coming in, referred to as "pipeline" income. For example, if you have a song on a recording that is already garnering airplay or selling records, mechanical and performance royalties are just waiting to be collected and paid to you. By doing a minimal amount of calculating, a publisher can make a ballpark estimate of how much you are likely to receive and then pay it to you as an advance. The publisher can offer such an advance without risking a cent because it's money that the song has already earned. Another scenario similar to pipeline income occurs if you are likely to generate publishing income in the very near future, such as when you have an artist deal or production deal in place. Again, such a deal lowers the publisher's risk.

Competition usually brings out the checkbooks, too. If two or more publishers are vying for your services as a writer, one of the enticements will be an advance. Bidding wars are legendary in the entertainment industry, so if you have the opportunity to be a seller of valuable services to two potential buyers with deep pockets, good for you. The respective companies' willingness to outbid each other will probably dictate the amount of your advance. If you are not the subject of a bidding war, I find the best formula for a fair advance is to do your homework: Put a pencil to paper and calculate what your true needs and wants are. These wants shouldn't include fantasies of having enough money to live an outrageous lifestyle in a mansion with a staff so you can write in peace or to purchase a yacht in Cancun. You want to prove that you are capable of understanding the publisher's business. Calculate a salary for yourself, studio and/or equipment costs, professional services (such as legal and accounting fees in connection with signing a publishing deal), any pressing debts, and other reasonable, identifiable costs. Chances are that the more detailed and businesslike you are, the more likely the publisher will be to take your requests seriously. I won't guarantee that everyone who presents a spreadsheet with a spending plan will get it all as an advance. However, such a presentation will cause your potential publisher to take you more seriously as a business partner and ally.

Whatever advance the publisher pays you directly or indirectly through a third party on your behalf, the publisher is entitled to *recoup* that money from your future earned royalties. That means you won't see any further money from the publisher until he makes back the amount of your advance. Once that is done, you start getting your share of the publishing royalties. Don't confuse recoupment with repayment. If you were obligated to repay the publisher, your financial arrangement would be characterized as a loan instead of an advance against royalties. Under the advance scenario, if your future royalties do not recoup the amounts that were advanced to you, the publisher has to chalk up the loss to making a bad business decision in signing you, advancing too much money on your behalf, not promoting your songs adequately, or some combination of them all.

The songwriter-publisher relationship is not the only type of relationship that you can enter into. One variation is the co-publisher relationship, where you and the publisher share ownership and duties regarding the exploitation of the songs in your catalog. In a co-publishing arrangement, not only will you receive your songwriting royalty, but a portion of the "publisher's share" of the earnings, as well. Another situation can be simply an administration agreement where you own your songs wholly and use the publisher to handle all of the administrative aspects of your copyrights. Some publishers are happy to collect a smaller percentage of the publishing revenue pie if it means being associated with a songwriter who is successful and savvy enough to create a publishing niche of his own.

Theme Variations: Timing Your Publishing Deal

One question that I am often asked is about the timing of a publishing deal: Should a combination recording artist/songwriter seek an artist deal before a publishing deal or vice versa? At the risk of sounding as if I'm avoiding a straight answer, there is no hard and fast rule here. It is all a matter of circumstances, including which deal leads to the other, how much you need the money, whether the two deals are directly tied into one another through one parent company, whether you really need to have a publisher, and other considerations. The more you know about what you want from either or both of these potential agreements, the better you can judge which one should come first, if at all.

Reversions, Revisions, and Restrictions

When negotiating a songwriter-publisher agreement, you should consider three other significant negotiation points. The first is the possibility of the reversion of songs that aren't exploited by the publisher. In this instance, there is an assumption that within a reasonable period of time, the publisher should be able to find uses for songs that were written during the term of the contract. If the publisher can't exploit the songs within this period of time, the ownership of the songs reverts back to the writer.

For both artistic and business reasons, you should take a very close look at granting a publisher the right to make revisions to your musical compositions. Songwriting is self-expression—there's no other way to put it. If you allow a publisher to revise your songs freely, the publisher can then change how you have expressed your inner feelings about things that mean a lot to you, like a love relationship or social issues. From the strictly business point of view, if the publisher has someone else make the revisions, your share of the song may be diminished to accommodate your new "collaborator." You might want to consider restricting revisions, either completely or only after you have had the opportunity to make the revisions first. In either event, you might want to limit how much of a share of a song to grant to a third-party collaborator if your publisher chooses one.

Finally, you may want to negotiate restrictions on how your publisher allows others to use your music. Some writers, for example, do not want their music used in political campaigns, alcohol advertisements, or violent or X-rated movies, or as samples. If you have a strong feeling about any use restrictions, it's a good idea to get it in writing.

These are only a few of the major points worth discussing with a potential music publisher if you are fortunate enough to be considered as a writer. Much like finding a record company as an artist, finding the right publisher is one of the most important decisions you can make in your career. Above all else, the ideal situation is to find a publisher who can sing at least two of your songs (don't laugh; some publishers will sign a writer without being able to identify or sing one song written by that writer). Even if you don't connect on the musical or artistic end, make sure that the publisher can articulate how he will increase the value of your catalog from the business and promotional perspective.

Music publishers are some of the most underrated executives and Artist and Repertoire (A&R) people in the music business. I find that people who go into the publishing side of the business are really passionate about songs and the people who write them. While you are researching opportunities to get a foothold in the industry, look for the names of publishers and individuals who work for publishers. Pay particular attention to liner notes from CDs, music trade magazines, and music business directories to get names of publishers.

One of the best ways to find out about publishers and the publishing business is to align yourself with one of the three U.S.-based performance rights organizations. Remember that the PROs—ASCAP, BMI, and SESAC—all have to know a little something about almost every music publisher in the business. Attending PRO-sponsored events and getting to know the writer/publisher representatives who work for PROs are great starting points.

Sample Clearance Agreement

A final agreement worth noting is a *sample clearance*. When sampling by using the actual recording of a piece of music and editing it, putting a different vocal or musical performance to it, or altering it in any way, you are technically breaching the sole right of the copyright holder to make a derivative or changed version of the original work unless you get permission from the original copyright holder to do so. Making this change with the copyright holder's blessing is called "clearing" the sample.

When clearing a sample, remember as discussed earlier that there may be two separate copyrights at issue—the PA copyright for the composition itself *and* the SR copyright for the master recording. Accordingly, be aware that you must contact the original music publisher to clear the musical composition, *and* contact the record company to clear the master recording of the song. Unless the music publisher and the record company are one and the same, you need to negotiate two separate agreements with the publisher and record company.

Each agreement should set forth who owns the new work that uses the original work, whether sampling the original will incur any fees, royalties, or advances against royalties, and how credits are to read on products that include the sample. Negotiation points include how much of the old work was used, how important and prominent it is to the new work, what kind of budget the artist and label supporting the artist might have, and timing of the negotiation. Clearing rights prior to the public release is always the best policy. Certainly, if an artist or label did not bother to clear a sample and it is being played on the radio and on television, and is released as a featured single from a recording, the owner of the original work that was sampled has a very strong negotiation position because of the threat of copyright infringement looming in the background. Fees and/or advances charged to those who sample can range from nominal amounts in the hundreds of dollars to several thousands of dollars, or recovery of the entire royalty stream, depending on the various factors already discussed.

If you consider sampling, the hiring of a lawyer or a sample clearance service that is well-versed in these matters is highly advised. Hiring an experienced lawyer is discussed in Chapter 12. Sample clearance services can be found through your network of industry contacts. Their fees vary on a case-to-case basis depending on the scope of the work you are hiring them for, the timing of when you hire them, and what the potential scope of the distribution of your project may be. Sampling can bring new life to old songs—both artistically and financially—and has become a major part of the music publishing landscape.

This brief introduction to the business of songwriting and music publishing is not by any means meant to be exhaustive. A number of academic music business programs have entire courses on the business of music publishing. Some great books have been written on the subject of music publishing, as well. I highly recommend that you research the field by picking up one or more of these books to learn even more about the subject.

Companion Questions

1. *Are you a writer who only writes songs, or a "writer plus" who writes songs and does something else such as recording, performing, or producing?*

2. *Do you write lyrics, music, or both? Do you like to work with a collaborator or have to work with a collaborator? How do you determine songwriting splits with your collaborators? Are you open to revising compositions after you have determined that they are finished? Are you headstrong about your creative ideas or open to suggestions?*

3. *How can a music publisher help you with your career? Is it to promote you and your songs? Is it to help you find an artist deal? Is it because you need the advance money? Is it to get you into markets that you are not currently working in (for*

example, are you a recording artist trying to break into film and television or a producer trying to find projects)?

4.   *What creative and technological tools do you need to write and produce demos on a consistent basis? If you don't currently have a demo of your songs, what is keeping you from making one?*

5.   *Can you write at a consistent pace for a long period of time? Do you write only when inspired? If so, will being obligated to write for a publisher affect your ability to be inspired to write?*

6.   *Does writing for money bother you? Can you write on demand or write for a specific project?*

7.   *Will you depend completely on your publisher to get your name known or are you willing to do some of the promotional efforts on your own? What kind of promotional efforts can you make now to expose yourself to A&R people and music consumers?*

8.   *Why do you write music? Is it something that you can do without?*

9.   *Who are some of your writing influences? What makes their music so great? What are you doing to improve your writing to reach the standards of your writing heroes?*

10.   *Are there professional organizations or support groups that you can join or form to share your songwriting with others? Do you make use of them?*

11.   *How do you deal with writer's block? Do you think having a music publisher will help you unblock or add to the pressure?*

12.   *Do you "write and edit"? Do you organically "jam" your way into a completed song? Do you lock the doors when writing and not come out until you have completed your work?*

4 Recording Artist Agreements

Most journeys into the unknown have a mythical Promised Land in the distance—a destination off in the horizon that can keep the traveler inspired and working toward it even when weary. In my experience, the Promised Land that many musicians share is known simply as "the Deal." The Deal is a goal, a target, a destination of grand proportions that the great musical stars have reached—a destination that awaits all who are willing to endure the journey.

This chapter of the *Musician's Legal Companion* is dedicated to all those who seek the Deal. I will do my best to demystify the Deal. I'll explain the parties involved in the Deal, introduce you to the variations of the Deal, and generally make you aware of the expectations and obligations of the various parties to the Deal. (Please note that for this chapter alone, I'm departing from my premise stated in Chapter 1 and am defining *musician* in the traditional sense, meaning a person who is proficient on a musical instrument.)

Hypothetical Situation: Record Deal or Prison Sentence?

Sherry has wanted to be a recording artist ever since she was 10 years old. She sang in high school musicals, trained with private vocal instructors, won a number of talent show competitions, and sang lead for a cover band. She picked up the guitar and started performing her own songs at open microphone showcases in her hometown. While performing some of her own songs at a showcase in Los Angeles, Sherry was approached by Paul, a songwriter/producer who had been working on developing a four-member, all-female group and was in search of a frontwoman. Paul told Sherry that she had "the look" for lead singer spot and asked whether she was interested in doing an audition along with the rest of the group for some "label people."

Not wanting to pass up any opportunity to make a connection, Sherry agreed to sing at the audition. She met the rest of the band for the first time three days before the audition and proceeded to learn a short set of heavily choreographed dancing while singing five songs written by Paul. While the material the group performed was not particularly challenging or what Sherry usually performs, writes, or even listens to, it was easy enough to learn and Sherry enjoyed dancing to it. The rehearsals were a great deal of work and very demanding. Between memorizing dance steps, lyrics, and music, Sherry had very little time to get to know the other members of the group beyond simply their first names. She was grateful that Paul was doing all the talking for the group.

Audition day came, and as promised by Paul, both the A&R and promotions team from a major label were in attendance at the club. The group performed an impressive set, and then had an opportunity to meet with all of the people from the label. Paul gathered the group together later to announce that the audition was successful, and they would be signed to a major label deal through his production company. The group, including Sherry, was ecstatic. Her break had arrived!

The next several weeks of Sherry's life were spent rehearsing new material written by Paul while negotiating the details of an exclusive artist deal with Paul's production company. Whenever the group's lawyer tried to make suggestions to revise the agreement, Paul accurately explained that his deal with the record label was already set, and they had given him very little room to make concessions to the group. They eventually signed the deal amid a certain amount of fanfare in the label's conference room with label staff in attendance and cheering as the contracts were signed. Sherry finally learned the rest of the group members' last names when she looked at the signature lines of the contract they signed.

Recording sessions started almost immediately, but did not require the artists' presence right away because Paul did all of the music writing and production on synthesized keyboards. Paul told the group that they could go their separate ways until he was ready for them. Sherry went back home to the Midwest and shared her good news with friends and family, using some of her portion of the group's advance money to live on. Three months later, the group eventually started singing their parts in the studio, learning the songs as they recorded. Some bickering and jealousy began to arise between group members. A great deal of the bitterness was directed at Sherry because she joined the group as the lead singer at the last second just before the deal was made, whereas the other members worked with Paul for over a year singing demos for him for free while holding down full-time jobs.

When Sherry asked about submitting material for the group's album, she was told that she didn't have the writing experience or track record that Paul has and that her songs didn't quite fit the genre of the group. They finished the lead-off single for the project and immediately started on a multi-city tour to promote the single, taking time between promotional dates to complete recording of the rest of the album. Since she was the lead singer and had a distinctive, attractive "look," Sherry was designated by the promotions department of the label as the spokesperson for the group, making the other members even more jealous. A year and a half after her initial audition, the album was finally released with a projected promotions timeline of another 18 months. During this combined three-year period, Sherry had been singing and would continue to sing songs that she really didn't like while traveling in close quarters with members of a group that didn't care for her. Taking into account the money that the label advanced to record and promote the project thus far, Sherry's group would have to sell at least 300,000 units before breaking even.

Background Material

At some point, you've changed your direction and moved beyond simply being a musician. The result of this change in your direction—whether deliberate or an outcome of revolution or evolution in your growth—is your perception of yourself as an artist. When a mechanical device such as a tape recorder or a digital recorder records that medium of self-expression, you are elevated to the status of a recording artist. In the legal context, the generally accepted definition of a "recording artist" is a musician who no longer simply plays music, but rather puts his or her own signature spin on it, adds a certain element of self-expression, and, of course, records it.

You take great pride in your artistry. You craft it, you practice it, you hone it. Eventually, you want to share recordings of your artistry with others. Maybe it is with a handful of others, maybe it is with millions. You may have made some recordings and given them away or maybe even sold them. However, you've come to the conclusion that a certain amount of time, effort, technical expertise, and energy is required to create, produce, and share these recordings. If you're like most artists I've met over the years, you would prefer to focus on the artistic side of your endeavors. And yet, unless you are independently wealthy, have a patron, or don't want or need to devote a great deal of your time to your efforts as a recording artist, you have to find some way of sustaining yourself financially as an artist.

"If only someone out there liked selling my music as much as I like making my music," you think to yourself, "I'd have more time to devote to my artistry and the world would be a better place." Well, someone does like selling music that much. Whether fueled by commerce, belief in an artist, or some combination of the two, that someone (or something) is what we've come to know as a record company. The idea of selling recordings of music to the public started back around the turn of the 20th century in the United States. The record companies of the time found that demand for recordings from a particular company increased when the public could buy recordings of an artist from only one particular company. From this practice came the concept of exclusive artist agreements. An artist would make recordings only for a certain company, so as the popularity of the artist grew, so did the profits of the company that owned the rights to the exclusive recording services of the artist. To reward the artist for this exclusivity, and as compensation for the artistic services rendered, the record companies paid a royalty to the recording artist based on recordings sold. Through the years, the companies and the industry have grown. The sophistication, details, and thus, the legalities of this basic arrangement between record company and artist have grown along with the industry over the past hundred years.

Companies that manufacture and distribute the recordings of artists have come, gone, grown, shrunk, and consolidated into the business structure of the recorded music industry that we've come to know today. As I write this book, deals are in the works for even further ownership changes with the largest of these companies. I will not identify any of them by name, because these changes are happening so quickly that any attempt by me to memorialize the information is likely to become obsolete almost immediately. However, it should be noted that a handful of large multinational companies with their beginnings in a variety of different businesses, from appliance rental to media to liquor distribution to high-tech electronics, have come to dominate the business of music distribution. These companies and their music subsidiaries are known as the major labels or "the majors." For our purposes, when an artist talks hopefully about the Deal, he is usually referring to signing an exclusive artist agreement with one of the majors or an affiliate company that is distributed by one of the majors. This is our starting point.

Before moving forward, I'd like to go over some vocabulary and roles first. *Being signed* is a phrase that I hear used quite a bit. It simply means that two parties have entered into a formal agreement for the artist's services. While many states honor the terms of oral agreements, an agreement of this magnitude is usually in writing; thus, the phrase "being signed." Indeed, a contract for services that spans greater than one year *must* be in writing to be binding and enforceable. A *label* or a *record label* is the trademark or name of the company that is generally responsible for the manufacture and distribution of recordings. *Record label* and *record company* are usually used interchangeably in conversation.

The role of the record company varies depending on whom you talk to, so it is a good idea to go through the entire spectrum of what the roles of a record label include. In large record companies, these roles are often separated into various departments, each with its own staff of employees. By looking at these departments one at a time, we can get an idea of where and how your artist deal fits into the overall process.

Artists usually have their initial contact with a division of a record company called the *A&R* department. A&R stands for artist and repertoire, meaning this department coordinates recording artists and the music that they record. The A&R department is primarily responsible for scouting talent—for example, stalking the clubs, listening to demos, and checking out contacts all over the country in search of acts that are compatible with the company. In addition, A&R departments work closely with the signed acts, interfacing with other departments within the company to create recordings that can be effectively marketed to the public. Depending on your style of music and how developed your act is, some labels have A&R reps in the studios with you to accept material from outside writers and publishers that they think might be good matches for your project and generally shepherd a recording along. Others take a completely hands-off approach, allowing you to do the bulk of your artist development and production on your own. Record companies also will take on the role of bankrolling the costs associated with the recording process. This includes paying for the entire range of projects from inexpensive, one-shot recording sessions to heavily produced projects that can take months or even years of time and rack up millions of dollars in recording costs.

Simply having a great single master recording isn't enough for most artists, though. To fuel a part-time or full-time career from your recording talents, you want other people to be able to hear and buy your music. Like any other product, your recording needs to be manufactured into a configuration that can be purchased. Over time, the so-called standard configuration of recorded music has changed based on a combination of consumer demand and what the record companies have to offer. Our industry has experienced an evolution, from sheet music; piano rolls; and 78, 45, and 33 rpm (revolutions per minute) phonograph records all the way to eight-track and cassette tapes; CDs; and the digital forms of music we have today. There are costs associated with the design, photography, printing, and mass production—elements that combined with the recorded media itself result in a product that the record company can sell. Record companies have traditionally taken on the financial responsibility of advancing these manufacturing costs, which eventually factor into overhead.

Next on the list of record company responsibilities is the distribution of these mass-produced recordings. They need to be spread around so a great number of consumers can be exposed to them and have an opportunity to buy them; otherwise, you simply have mass-produced versions of a great recording that sit in boxes on a shelf. The major record labels have developed a distribution network of their own, which enables them to get recorded music into retail stores. Wholly separate from the major label distribution system is the independent network of record distributors that have similar relationships with retailers.

Finally, a demand needs to be created for the sales of the recordings. While an artist can generate a great deal of this demand by performing live, the promotional efforts of a record label are crucial and often necessary to gain mass consumer exposure. Traditionally, a combination of radio, press, online media, and advertising promotions is used to create audience awareness and excitement for artists. Using in-house personnel or hiring third parties, record companies create the campaigns that transform unknown artists into household names.

All of the preceding responsibilities form the backdrop and starting point of a label's position in a relationship with you, the artist. Some labels bring more experience, personnel, money, and other resources to this relationship; some bring less. Some artists bring more of their own audience, money, reputation/name recognition, press, and other resources to this relationship; some bring less. While these relative bargaining positions dictate many of the high-profile financial details of the artist–record company agreement, including artist advances, royalties, and bonuses, we need to focus our discussion on the basic artist–label relationship. The record company has the experience and resources to broaden your audience and sell recordings. You have the talent and desire to be heard by a broader audience. Both sides seek to earn enough money from this relationship to enable them to keep doing it. Oversimplified? Maybe. The essence of the relationship? You bet. That's our basic starting point.

You might argue, "But I can do all that stuff myself. I don't need a record company to do all this for me and take all my money!" This argument has become increasingly valid, especially as technology has developed and enabled artists to handle a great deal of the label responsibilities. If this is your firm and unwavering belief, then my advice is to not get into a relationship with a third-party record company and start working immediately to get your music heard. However, before you make such a drastic decision, think about what you might gain from having someone else take on the various responsibilities that this section has discussed. By far, the two most important tangible advantages that you gain when a third party takes on any or all of these duties are the time and expense involved in carrying out these duties. If someone else is handling these responsibilities, it frees up your time and resources—financial and otherwise—to devote to your artistry. It takes time and money to develop the skill set, contacts, and sales strategies necessary to produce, manufacture, and market the work of a recording artist effectively. Only you can decide in your heart if this aggregate time and financial investment is worth sharing the wealth with someone else. If you decide it is worthwhile to enter into a relationship with a record company, this section has laid the foundation for discussing some of the major issues that you may want to consider as you negotiate the terms of your relationship.

Exclusive versus Non-exclusive

A major consideration of recording agreements is whether your relationship with the record company is exclusive. The record company wants the relationship to be exclusive. The company is making a substantial financial investment in producing and promoting your music, and thus wants that investment to be reflected in the sales of its products, not the sales of a competing company. In a perfect world, the artist's relationship with the record company is symbiotic. If your name and reputation should become more valuable due to the company's efforts, then the company's name will likewise become more valuable.

It is relatively common for an artist to have a non-exclusive relationship with a record company. Single-record or "one-off" deals do exist in the industry. The advantage is that you can still be a free agent, giving you the flexibility to look for another record company in the future if it would prove to be a better fit. For example, you might make a one-off deal with a small, regional record company with limited promotional resources. If the company takes the approach that this recording is the only one it will have with you and it had better give it the company's best shot, then you're in pretty good shape. The added efforts put into your recording might be the thing that attracts larger labels with more money, experience, and wider promotional range than the regional label can offer. Then, you may be in a great position to choose either to make a deal with one of the larger companies that didn't know about you before, make another, similar deal with the smaller company with the advantage of knowing how you work with each other, or anything in between. A potential disadvantage of the one-off deal is that absent an exclusive relationship, a company might not work as hard on your project as it would on another artist signed to the company with whom the company has a more committed relationship. With a one-off deal, if the record company doesn't promote your recording as well due to the non-exclusivity of your arrangement, perhaps the record would not attract the attention of other companies, leaving you with fewer options.

Compilation records are very popular hybrids of non-exclusive and exclusive relationships between artists and record companies. Record companies that own the exclusive recording rights of certain artists can contract with the company putting together the compilation and for a flat fee, royalty, or some combination of the two, allow the compiling company to license (borrow) the masters as well as the right to use the artist's name in connection with the sale of the compilation. These arrangements usually have a "courtesy credit" provision so the public makes the connection between the artist and the original company with which the artist has an exclusive relationship. Many times, non-exclusive artists are also included on the same compilation recordings as exclusive artists, which gives lesser-known artists the opportunity to be associated with major label artists on the same project.

A company that owns exclusive rights to an artist can also license (loan) out his or her services to perform on other projects, either as a non-featured performer (such as being a session instrumentalist or vocalist) or as a featured guest artist. In the case of the background artist, you simply would be listed in the credits like any other session player or vocalist along with a courtesy credit (for instance, "Joe Guitarist appears courtesy of XYZ Records"). If you are appearing as a featured performer, which means that your performance, name, and reputation are being used as a selling point for that particular recording, the company that owns your exclusive rights as a recording artist could ask for payment of a fee, a piece of the royalty from the project, or other negotiated compensation from the record company of the artist with whom you are appearing.

Both the compilation and the featured artist configurations have become commonplace in the industry. It is a way for you and your record company to cross-promote effectively. It should be noted, however, that the timing of releases is very important for all involved, as cross-promoting projects at the same time to the same audience may leave you in competition with yourself or diminish your audience popularity due to overexposure.

Contract or Lockdown?

In cases of exclusivity, a major question that arises with any contract—including artist deals, songwriting deals, endorsement deals, and others—is the length of your exclusivity. Most traditional major label contracts consist of an initial contract period followed by a series of option periods, with the opportunity to exercise the option being granted solely to the record company. At a time when major label artists release recordings only every two or sometimes even three years, a five-album deal can have you wrapped up for at least 10 years! This extraordinary length of service can certainly be viewed as against public policy. For example, there have been attempts in the California legislature to limit personal service contracts to seven years. To avoid a controversy for not delivering the minimum number of albums within the allowable time frame, it is advisable to have an experienced entertainment lawyer advise you on the legal duration for contract obligations in your jurisdiction. As with any relationship, if everything is going great, a decade can fly by in a snap, but if either side is dissatisfied with the relationship, being under contract for that length of time could be pure hell.

Before you assume that signing such a contract is the equivalent of being shackled to a ball and chain for the rest of your natural life, consider the rationale for this logic. The record company is taking a considerable risk with you and their other artists; it is not guaranteed that every recording it releases will make a significant return on its investment. To recoup the sizable cost of developing and promoting a new artist, as well as to offset the money that it loses on acts that don't make it, the company needs to be able to benefit from its signings over several years and projects. The time it takes to release and promote five albums still sounds like a long time, doesn't it?

One solution is to make the record company's exercise of the options contingent upon the payment of cash advances or meeting certain performance levels, such as guaranteed releases, promotion commitments, or tour support. The advances are usually the most common middle ground; if an act is making money for the record company or if the company really believes in the act, it is well worth the option costs for the company to continue the relationship.

Creative Control

Some artists spend years creating their own trademark sound, assembling the right combination of songs, figuring out who they like to work with, and developing a method for transforming this melting pot of creativity into something that a record company can sell. Other artists have never been in a recording studio in their lives, don't write songs, and have never explored their own musical identity. Depending on where you fit between these two extremes, the issue of creative control of your recordings will either be something that you ferociously fight for or graciously give up. Many record companies, citing that they are protecting their investment in your act, will want to have a great deal of creative control over your project. This includes details like choice of studio, budget, producer, musical genre, what material you perform, and other creative calls, all the way up to having the final approval of what is considered to be a commercially acceptable recording, and which songs are actually included on the record. A combination of careful negotiating of recording procedures, coupled with building a spirit of trust and sharing ideas, is the recommended method for alleviating issues of creative control.

The best method by far of gaining as much creative control as possible over your projects is to walk into the relationship with a clear vision of who you are as an artist and the chops to back it up. What I'm suggesting is that you do a great deal of your artist development on your own, which is a huge responsibility. This may not be your absolute ideal situation, but it is the trade-off for artistic freedom, and creates a relationship with a record company that is less likely to end up with you having to wrest away control of your sound down the road.

Promotional Commitments

Negotiating a commitment from your record company to promote your recordings can enhance your chances of shared success. While not exhaustive, here is a brief list of some of the promotional efforts to which record companies are willing to commit: setting aside specific dollar amounts for promotions; distributing releases in specific territories; video production; radio promotion; hiring a publicist; and tour support. The difficulty lies in what you as an artist can reasonably request or even plan for early on in your relationship with a record company. As you formulate plans for how you want your career to unfold, share them with your label to see how your plans can intersect with the label's promotional efforts.

Of course, one of the main obligations that you must commit to as an artist is to make yourself available for promotional appearances. These range from simple in-store autograph sessions to full-blown concerts. Many artists are not prepared for the great deal of time it takes to travel from town to town, shaking hands at radio stations and retail stores, sounding relatively alive while doing 7 a.m. interviews, and opening up their lives via the media in an effort to sell their recordings. Whether or not you are on a major label, these appearances are all necessary to promote your products, so be ready to take on the responsibility of promotions when deciding to become a recording artist.

Royalties and Advances

The issue of artist royalties has always been one of the major negotiation points of artist–record company agreements. I've found that working my way with a client through the forest of percentage points, reductions, deductions, returns, reserves, and other financial terms of a major label agreement is often a harrowing exercise. With this in mind, I would like to review the basics of the traditional recording artist royalty structure using very conservative and easy-to-follow numbers. While the standards for royalty rates are changing constantly as artist production contribution and digital distribution practices evolve, a basic understanding of the concepts discussed below are important to grasp.

Let's begin with a clear understanding of artist royalties. When I refer to an *artist royalty* in this discussion, it is specifically the royalty paid to the recording artist solely for providing services as a recording artist. Artist royalties should not be confused with mechanical royalties (discussed in the previous chapter) that may be earned by a recording artist who also writes her own material. Remember that these two royalties (artist royalties and mechanical royalties) are separate royalties paid for separate services. I find that the confusion arises because (1) sometimes the artist providing each service is the same person, and (2) both royalties are based on the sales of the same recordings. Separating the apples from the oranges (the recording artist services from writing services) will be helpful. Sometimes, however, an artist might be the producer of Masters as well, in which case the combined artist-producer royalty is paid to the artist. When this is the case, the combined royalty is referred to as an "all-in" producer-artist royalty. Since both of these royalties are being paid to the artist, for simplification purposes of this example, I will refer to this all-in royalty as an artist royalty as well.

Artist royalties are traditionally based on either the suggested retail price of a recording or the wholesale price that a record company charges to retailers or distributors. Between the fluctuating prices that different retail stores charge for the same product, and consumer demand driving down the cost of recordings, basing royalties on the suggested retail price of a record can be an unstable deal. Using a wholesale price base will give the deal some stability; however, adjustments need to be made in order to get the same rate when comparing wholesale and retail royalties. While most artists and their record companies protect the information about their royalty rates like the combination to a bank vault, it is generally accepted that the retail-price royalty range for major label artist fluctuates between 8 percent for unknown artists with very little negotiating clout and more than 20 percent for superstar artists with a track record. Wholesale royalties are adjusted according to what each respective record company charges to stores.

Let's take as an illustration a royalty rate somewhere in the middle of this range. If you were to negotiate a deal for 12 percent of the retail rate and the suggested retail price of your recordings is $15, then your base rate would be $1.80 per unit. If the wholesale price for that same recording is $7.50 (a 50 percent reduction in the retail rate), the adjusted artist royalty would be 24 percent of the wholesale price (a 100 percent increase from the retail rate). If you sold 50,000 units, you'd be sitting pretty at $90,000, right? Well, not so fast; let's look at some additional accounting first.

Recoupable Costs

Our artist royalties calculations need to be considered next to recoupable costs. Over time, record companies have developed a number of costs that are billed back to artists and recouped from sales of records. While these recoupable costs are negotiable, some of them have become accepted as relatively standard in the normal course of business. Recording costs—including studio rental, outside musicians, vocalists, producer fees, and engineer fees—are all recoupable expenses. Often, video costs and outside radio promotional costs are recoupable. For both video and radio promotion, the recoupable amount varies from 50 percent to 100 percent of the actual costs. Artist advances and monies spent on the artist's behalf (such as promotional trips for the press or monies paid to third parties on the artist's account) and tour support are recoupable as well.

Both artists and labels are taking advantage of the modern Do It Yourself (DIY) world with artists being able to produce and deliver world-class audio recordings, video recordings, and a great deal of ready-to-use promotional materials to record labels. These costs may not be subject to recoupment at all or, in the alternative, kept to a minimum. However, as you can imagine, if money is being wildly spent and left unchecked, these recoupable costs can quickly add up. Think about that the next time you see some superstar jetting around to some foreign country to promote a record or to lay a vocal track on a single; the record company is recouping the expense of the jet.

Now, to be absolutely fair, we're not talking about outrageous amounts of money being spent on every single project, so don't stereotype all of the record companies as being guilty of wild and excessive spending. Looking at our previous example, let's plug in a few more conservative but realistic dollar amounts. Let's attribute $60,000 to recording costs; two singles promoted to radio at a cost of $45,000 each (at 50 percent recoupment); accompanying videos for the two singles at $75,000 apiece (at 50 percent recoupment); $20,000 in tour support to buy some gear, rent a truck, and pay for side musicians and hotels; and $20,000 each to the three band members as an artist advance. Even with these conservative figures, the recoupable amount for this project is $260,000.

Royalties Revisited

Continuing with our example, the label still needs to make some accounting adjustments before putting money into our artist's pockets. Artist royalties usually include any royalties paid to third parties such as outside producers (note the "all-in royalty" discussed above). If a 3 percent royalty is paid to producers in our example (a reduction of 25 percent of the artist's royalty), the net artist royalty actually is now down to $1.35 per unit. Labels then make adjustments for a variety of reasons, including breakage, packaging deductions, and a variety of other deductions until one by one, the negotiated artist royalty is whittled down to a fraction of what originally was negotiated. Let's assume that the combined amount of the previously described deductions is 10 percent of the net artist rate (again, this is a conservative figure).

After the label makes all of these adjustments, at 50,000 units, instead of the $90,000 in artist royalties that we anticipated, your artist royalties end up being dramatically different. The first thing we need to do is to subtract the third-party producer royalty of $22,500 (3 percent of $15 or 45 cents multiplied by 50,000 units) from artist royalties. This leaves a net artist royalty of $67,500 ($90,000 minus $22,500). The 10 percent combined deductions reduce the royalty by $6,750, leaving a figure of $60,750. The recoupable expenses included artist advances of $60,000 ($20,000 for each of the three band members), recording costs of $60,000, video productions costs of $75,000 (50 percent of two videos at $75,000 apiece), radio promotions costs of $45,000 (50 percent of two singles at $45,000 each), and $20,000 in tour support. Subtracting all of these recoupable expenses (totaling $260,000) from the adjusted artist royalty, instead of being paid $90,000, you would still be unrecouped in the amount of $199,250. While your label does not require that you write it a check for that amount to pay it back, you still have to sell quite a few units to even approach receiving royalties.

At 50,000 units, this band is still close to $200,000 in the hole. On the up side, each of the band members has seen $20,000 in artist advances and maybe picked up some gear from the tour support. But the fact remains that the band still has to sell quite a few records—more than an additional 150,000—for the band and the record company to break even. Once again, I want to emphasize that these are very conservative figures and are not intended to scare you away from major record companies. It is, however, meant to illustrate the reality that the stakes are very high when it comes to the kinds of sales that major record companies are expecting from the acts they sign. Unfortunately, the reality of the major label world has become that only those artists who sell a lot of records can recoup the significant investment made by the record companies.

Alternatives: Independent Record Companies

The good news is that major labels are not the only game in town. While many of the same issues previously discussed are shared by smaller, independent record companies, the independents have a few advantages worth noting. First, independents are usually working on a much smaller scale than majors, and thus spend less money. If you were counting on paying for a new sports car with your artist advance, the independents' budgets may not be to your liking. On the other hand, the smaller budget might be in your favor because the recoupable expenses are much lower than with a major, thus the pressure to sell really big numbers is decreased. Be it by genre or geography, independent labels also tend to have more focused niches than major record companies do. This means there is less of a chance that money will be spent without focus, the marketing effort will be more targeted, and the audience is likely to be more loyal. This great combination of advantages can enable a label with limited resources, and the artists on that label, to succeed.

Alternatives: Production Agreements

Another alternative is signing an exclusive artist agreement with a production company. Production companies are different from record companies because even though they produce the master recordings just as record labels do, production companies stop short of the manufacture and distribution of the recordings that they make. Many independent production companies fill the role formerly served by the A&R departments at record companies. The production companies seek out talent, sign the artists to multiyear production agreements at a certain royalty rate, provide the skill and expertise to develop the acts, and then sell the acts off to record companies at a price "marked up" from the original royalty rate. This is a win-win situation because the producers are more aware of "the street" than the record company can be, the producers are taking care of the artist development at their own expense, and the record companies can hand-pick the acts that fit their company profiles with much less risk than if the label signed the artist from scratch.

Alternatives: Development Deals

Both major and independent record companies sign artists to development deals, which are basically equivalent to a test drive of the artists. The recording industry adopted this concept from the film and television business. In this variation of the artist deal, a company signs the artist to an abbreviated exclusivity period (for example, six months instead of a year or longer) during which the artist commits to recording demos funded by the company. The demos gives the record company an idea of the direction of the artist's work and how the artist works in the studio, and allows the company an opportunity to observe the working habits and ethic of the artist. If, after reviewing the demos, the record company decides it wants to work with the artist, then it converts the development deal into a long-term artist relationship as described previously. If the record company decides to pass on the artist, the artist has a demo to let other record companies listen to in order to try to get an artist deal.

The ability of artists to secure direct distribution arrangements, to sell products directly to their audiences, and the explosion of digital distribution opportunities have collectively forced both independent and major record labels to be creative and flexible when it comes to crafting an exclusive "Deal." Variations of what used to be a relatively standard agreement of "time and money" now offer flexibility when it comes to shortening the term of exclusivity, changing the delivery requirements, expanding or contracting the "rights package" obtained from the artist, giving the artist more creative control, alternative royalty structures, and more. The creativity of the deal-makers is now being tested with the restructuring of the entertainment industry and the business savvy of artists.

As this book goes to the printer, a new twist to the exclusive artist recording deal is developing with mixed implications. Dubbed the "360 degree deal," this exclusive artist agreement entails that a company secures all of the rights that an artist has to offer, including recording rights, songwriting/publishing rights, management rights, merchandising rights, and performance rights, in exchange for a share in the artist's income. As the name implies, this type of deal takes into account all 360 degrees of an artist's talents and earning capacity when securing rights. While some view the 360 deal as an innovative partnership between artist and industry that works for established artists who are paid significant advances for their complete services, others are criticizing the deal as a "land grab" of rights—a throw back to the "old days" of presenting 360 deals as a "take it or leave it proposition" that exploits inexperienced artists who do not have a grasp on how valuable their services are. Only time will tell if the 360 degree deal will become a standard of exclusive artist agreements. As you proceed in your career, do so with caution and evaluate the pros and cons of "packaging" yourself prematurely.

As you can see, the Deal is no longer simply one mythical destination. Necessity and innovation have turned what used to be only one choice into many for artists and record companies alike. Many artists are making conscious choices to be associated with smaller, more targeted companies largely because they allow the artists to have more control over their careers. In addition, the corporate structure and spending of major record companies are forcing artists to try to generate hundreds of thousands of sales. Many artists no longer want to face such pressure and are opting to seek other opportunities, professional paths, and relationships that lead them closer to their goals. Ultimately, it is important for artists to understand how, where, and to what degree the sales of recorded music fits into their careers. They can then put that relationship in the right priority and develop their own version of the Deal from there.

Companion Questions

1. *What attributes do you think make an artist special? Name three artists whom you feel are good examples of the artist you'd like to grow into and list what you like about them. Why?*

2. *Name a recording/distribution company that you like and why. Who are some of the artists associated with that company? What has the company done for those artists that you would like a similar company to do for you? Have you researched the ownership and executive makeup of the various entertainment companies to decide which one is the best match for you?*

3. *Do you like selling yourself to the public? If a music recording/ distribution company were to ask you how you would help it market your recordings, what would you say that you could*

do to help? Would you perform live in multiple territories? Would you be willing to do a series of radio interviews or in-studio shows? Can you deal with the intrusion on your private life due to press and public relations efforts trying to make you a household name?

4. How much creative control do you need to have over your own project? Would you exchange artistic control and the concept of your image for sales?

5. Do you feel the need to see a quick return on your investment of time and effort as an artist in the form of advances or royalties? Have you positioned yourself to make a demand for advances from a music–based company? How?

6. Have you already developed into an artist you feel is ready to be shared with the public or are you in need of artist development? Do you have the plan or the means to develop yourself as an artist?

7. List 10 musical recordings that changed your life. What was so great about them? Are you capable of changing someone's life with your recordings? Do you aspire to do so? Why?

8. Do you need to see or hear your work on a large scale to be more personally satisfied?

9. How many years of your career would you like to devote to recording music? How many recordings would you like to make in that time?

5 Artist-Management Agreements

From Colonel Tom Parker's hand-holding of Elvis Presley during the infancy of the pop music business in the 1950s to the guidance of artists through the highly sophisticated multimedia industry of today, the personal manager is the mastermind that assembles and holds an artist's team of professionals together. It is no secret that the success or failure of any business—no matter how big or small—rests largely on the talent, desire, ambition, and experience of the management team running it. It is especially the case in the music industry where the intersection of creativity, emotion, and business needs to be addressed on a day-to-day basis. In my opinion, the artist-manager relationship is by far the most important relationship in our industry.

In such an important relationship, a variety of legal issues need to be considered when artist and manager alike consider taking the plunge to work together as a team. The manager's role in an artist's career is so complex that it would be useless for me simply to dive into the various clauses of a "standard" artist-manager contract without first giving an overview of the artist-manager relationship.

In this brief introduction to the manager's role in an artist's career, I will discuss the distinct phases and details of the artist-manager relationship: development, payment, packaging, industry promotion, expansion, and exit strategies, as well as the major contract points of an artist-manager agreement. Each area has a variety of legal issues for you to consider that I will discuss, as well. After we've looked at all of the components of the relationship in this manner, we can then look at some of the other basic agreement issues.

Hypothetical Situation: The Management Maze

Singer-songwriter Arnie Artist outgrew the small town in Texas where he was raised and struck out on his own in the music business. He played guitar in a cover band for five years, an experience that did wonders to develop his stage presence and ear for hit songs. Arnie received plenty of encouragement and friendly advice along the way from people who told him how great he would be when he finally "made it." One friend, Morty, who used to play in a band with Arnie, wanted to hit the big time, too, as a businessman. Morty and Arnie promised each other that neither of them would leave the other behind.

After he moved to Los Angeles, Arnie made valuable contacts in the entertainment industry. He got to know other singer-songwriters as he made the rounds doing open microphone nights and offered his services to producers as a background vocalist for recording sessions while waiting tables at night. One day while in a studio singing background vocals at a recording session for a very successful record producer, Arnie was introduced to the producer's manager, Bobby, a veteran music executive and freelance consultant for major record labels. The two of them hit it off very well. Bobby offered to teach Arnie the business and open some doors for him, "with no strings attached," as Bobby put it.

True to his word, over the next year, Bobby made himself available to Arnie whenever Arnie had a question about business practices in the industry. Bobby occasionally invited Arnie to industry conventions, award shows, and parties, introducing Arnie to influential industry executives as "his new discovery." Bobby also provided Arnie access to recording studios, producers, and musicians, who all helped Arnie put together a professional demo of his original songs for free because of their relationship with Bobby. Bobby told Arnie that there were still no strings attached professionally, but when it seemed as though Arnie's career was ready to take off, they could then "work out their arrangement." Arnie agreed, telling Bobby that he was very grateful for the career direction and wanted to repay him for it some day.

Meanwhile, Morty made a few contacts of his own in the industry by moving to Nashville, where he enrolled in a college that offered music business courses. He got an internship with Zach, an experienced manager who traded time between Nashville and New York. Bobby and Morty stayed in touch throughout this year, sharing their newfound knowledge, contacts, and mutual excitement as they kept each other abreast of their progress in the business. Morty even managed to convince Zach to use Arnie to open up for some of his firm's clients when they played smaller venues close to Los Angeles. Zach told them that he liked what he saw in them—talent and loyalty. Zach started to talk to some of his record label contacts about Arnie and Morty.

One day, Arnie got a call from Mr. Bigger, a record company executive and former business partner of Bobby. Bigger was given Arnie's demo by Carrie Connection, a personal friend of Bigger. Carrie saw Arnie perform at a club and was very impressed. Mr. Bigger told Arnie that he wanted to offer him a record deal immediately as long as Carrie would get the job as Arnie's manager. Bobby angrily called Arnie a few hours later and wanted to know what was going on with their relationship because Bigger was telling everyone in L.A. about his new discovery. Bobby threatened to "ruin" Arnie if he made the Bigger-Connection deal. A few days later, Morty called Arnie because Zach heard through the grapevine about the Mr. Bigger deal and wanted to know if Arnie was open to other offers from his contacts. Zach offered to give Morty a full-time job if Morty signed up Arnie as a client so the two of them could co-manage Arnie's career.

After years of waiting for his break, Arnie found himself wishing for the simple life again.

Development

The earliest phase of the artist-manager relationship is one of development. This period includes the development of talent, development of communication patterns, development of business systems, and—most of all—the development of a solid overall artist-manager relationship. Usually, the artist and manager are getting to know one another, what each other's strengths and weaknesses are, and how they work together.

Our industry has changed dramatically in the last decade due to a number of factors that have converged at the time of this book, resulting in an even greater need for a management team that can work closely with an artist to develop and implement a solid career plan. The first of these factors is the availability of technology that allows the production of high-quality recordings of music at a relatively low cost. In addition, technology has been developed that allows these music recordings and the artist's image to be distributed worldwide to the public immediately.

At the same time, what we used to refer to as "the record business" has evolved (and continues to evolve) into a much broader multimedia entertainment business in which the role of the major, well-funded record labels is primarily to distribute and market talent that has already been "pre-developed." The combination is a double-edged sword because, on one hand, an artist can naturally and organically develop into the musician of his or her choice. On the other hand, the experience and guidance of the development process that used to be one of the most important and creative roles of major record labels is almost extinct. The days of A&R executives and talent scouts discovering and signing large numbers of unknown artists, songwriters, and garage bands in the infancy of their careers on a hunch that they have pure talent, and then nurturing those artists into fruition, are just about gone.

Most young artists are inexperienced at developing their talent, so often they lack the luxury to step back and be objective about the time it takes and the incremental benchmarks to look for as they hone their skills. In addition, while an artist nurtures their talent, they need to develop a relationship with the industry as well as find an audience. It has been my observation that these duties and responsibilities fall squarely on the shoulders of the personal manager much more now than ever before.

During this critical phase, the manager's primary role is to identify the artist's talents, objectively evaluate them, and then assist in the artist's development of those talents in a logical order and pace. This also works on the other side of the relationship, as well. An artist should use this time to pay particular attention to the strengths and weaknesses of the manager. Is the manager good with people or abrasive? Do they have good organization skills? Are you motivated to work, and will others be motivated to work for you because of this manager? Is this manager honest? Do they share responsibilities with you or do they try to control you?

At this early stage, some managers will demand the execution of an exclusive contract prior to taking any actions at all on behalf of an artist. In my experience, there is no particular profile of a manager who will ask for the signature on the dotted line this early in the relationship. I've seen managers with no experience at all want to secure their arrangement for fear of being left out of a deal, as well as big-time experienced managers who want the deal closed early in the relationship because they believe that the artist needs their experience and phone book of connections. The timing of when to sign an exclusive management contract will be discussed later in this chapter, but be aware that you may be faced with making the decision pretty early on. I usually advise artist clients to err on the side of caution and put off the "early decision" until the relationship seasons to a point of comfort on both sides. In most cases, if you, as an artist, continue to develop and grow, the manager will not abandon the relationship.

The way the development stage unfolds largely depends on the level of your talent and career at the time you meet the manager. For example, a 30-year-old musician with a catalog of published songs, seasoned by years of gigs and studio session work, requires a lot less hand-holding than a very talented 14-year-old novice musician with little or no experience who needs to grow up as a teenager/young adult as well as an artist. Sometimes managers are very actively involved in the development process, suggesting schooling and coaches, assembling musicians, producers, and co-writers for you to work with, and overseeing the creation, development, and coordination of every facet and person involved with your entire act. This "dream team" approach proved extremely effective with the development of the classic Motown artists in the 1960s and has been replicated on reality television shows that depict a "boot camp" approach to artist development.

Other managers take a more hands-off approach to artist development, allowing you to develop at your own pace. For example, The Beatles did a great deal of their growing up, both artistically and personally, in a crucial development year prior to meeting their legendary manager, Brian Epstein. During this time, the group traveled between England and Germany, playing several sets a night several nights a week at clubs. The group really didn't need to have a manager watching them develop from day to day as they grew into the people, performers, and songwriters that the world eventually came to know. It is my opinion that the fact that they didn't have someone to chaperone them as young men looking for adventure and keep them out of trouble is probably a major reason that they developed as quickly as they did as artists and as people.

You need to decide what works best for you when it comes to development. If it is important for you to work with someone who has the professional objectivity to provide you with feedback, motivation, direction, and organization, let the manager know that you want and need their input. If you are independent, self-motivated, have good practice habits, and can objectively evaluate yourself, then let the manager know that a hands-off approach is best, and that they need only check in with you periodically. What is crucially important during this phase is for the artist and manager to agree upon a relatively objective level of competency for the artist to reach before the artist is to be introduced to the rest of the industry.

The subjective nature of the development phase of the artist-manager relationship makes the legal issues involved difficult to reduce to an objective form. While it is possible to find the right words to draft a contract, the interpretation of those words can be wide open. After all, how much coaching and encouragement are too little or too much? Can an artist nullify a contract because the manager didn't supervise rehearsals? Can a manager claim a breach of contract because the artist isn't practicing according to a given schedule? As you can see, the relationship and communication between the parties are going to be key in interpreting how the parties' agreements with each other are interpreted.

Paying the Piper

How and how much to pay an artist manager are two of the greatest questions in the music industry. News stories of unsavory managers making off with millions of dollars from successful artists often make inexperienced artists extremely wary of would-be managers asking for a piece of the pie. Fortunately, compensation to managers is also completely negotiable, so with some creativity and business acumen, the parties involved can hopefully come up with a fair and realistic result.

One form of payment to a manager can be to pay them to provide management duties on an hourly basis. Artist and manager just need to negotiate a fair hourly fee, how often the billing will occur, and to clearly define what duties and activities can be billed to the artist. A variation on this compensation would be to hire the manager on a retainer basis. In this scenario, the manager is hired for a set fee (usually weekly or monthly) with minimum expectations for what the manager is supposed to accomplish within a particular time frame.

Most often, managers are paid from the artist's entertainment business earnings. The percentage that the manager is paid is referred to as a *manager's commission*. This is a very fair and logical payment arrangement when you think about it. The artist wants to create and/or increase income from the entertainment industry, and the manager's job is to guide the artist in how to earn that income. If they both do their jobs correctly, the manager is paid from the earnings that they and the artist generated from their work together. Three major points are to be discussed when paying a manager on a percentage basis: How much should the percentage be? How do the parties define the artist's income on which the percentage will be based? How long does the manager get to collect this commission?

The amount of the management commission varies widely. Some managers donate their time and efforts with no expectation of return simply because they want artist to succeed; others have earned up to a reported 50 percent of the artist's gross income. The common figures I've seen in the industry are from 10 to 20 percent of the gross income of the artist. When arriving at a figure, consider the number of people involved in the act (an eight-person group paying a manager 20 percent of its gross ends up rewarding the manager more than any single person in the group earns); whether the act is already earning money in the business (why should a manager be rewarded by commissioning the first $100,000 of your income if you already have been earning that amount without the manager?); and whether the manager is devoting all of their time to your act.

Determining the basis of the management commission can also be tricky. Most managers want to base their commission on gross receipts, meaning every dollar earned by an act is subject to the management commission. On one hand, basing the commission on the gross makes the calculations easier and can serve to prevent "creative accounting" on the artist's side to deny the manager hard-earned money. On the other hand, artists sometimes have high overhead such as touring expenses, recording expenses, and similar costs, so why should the manager be paid based on money that the artist wouldn't receive anyway? One way to address this issue is to pay the manager on a net basis. Calculating a "net commission base" is accomplished by reducing the gross receipts by certain agreed costs (for example, touring costs or record production costs) that the artist incurs in the course of doing business. For the parties to calculate a fair net basis for commissions, they both have to be familiar with the reasonable business costs of the artist. A record producer has very different costs than a performing artist, and they both have very different costs than a session singer or player. Once again, good communication and a certain level of industry knowledge on both sides will assist in coming to a fair commission base.

The last component of the management commission is how long the commission will be paid. On the management side, the logic is that participation should last forever for any products created or deals structured during the time that the manager worked for the artist. Many managers feel this is fair because the hard work and connections that created the opportunity for those products and deals are valuable enough to be rewarded perpetually. Under such a commission structure, if the artist writes or records any songs during the term of the artist-management relationship, the manager participates in the exploitation of those works well beyond the term of the relationship. Artists and their representatives often argue that managers should participate only for the period of time that they are directly involved with the artist; thus, when the relationship ends, the right to commissions ends, as well. A *sunset clause* is a contractual concept often employed as a compromise to these two very different payment structures. This type of arrangement provides for a diminishing commission to the manager after the contract term ends (for example, from 15 percent to 10 percent to 5 percent in consecutive years).

As you can see, valuation of the combination of a manager's skill, contacts, commitment, and overall importance to a musician's career is not an easy calculation. However, by working together to develop a well-thought-out and realistic plan using real numbers to project an artist's potential earnings, the basic terms for a fair financial reward can be crafted for a manager who can effectively deliver what the artist needs to make a successful career.

Packaging

After development, the artist's initial demo is one of the manager's most important tools to introduce the artist to the industry and the public. The manager's primary role during this phase of an artist's career is to help the artist identify which business opportunities should be pursued and then tailor the artist's package accordingly. Traditionally, on the music side of the entertainment business, an artist who was seeking a record contract in the past would put together a package most commonly consisting of a three- to four-song demonstration in the form of a non-commercial recording in the current industry standard medium (known as the "artist demo"), a photo that presents an idea of the artist's image, and biographical material. Because of industry access to artists via the Internet—particularly through entertainment sites that include self-made videos and social networking sites—a video presentation, now known as an Electronic Press Kit (EPK), is an essential part of the manager's promotions arsenal.

Many artists prefer to release a Master Recording for sale to the public to use as a demonstration. This is a major decision that the artist and manager need to discuss in detail from many points of view—including whether or not the artist or the manager is ready to physically, artistically, financially, or emotionally devote the time and effort to run an independent label when all they really want to do is have a demonstration package to show to people. A more complete discussion of what to consider when making an independent label release can be found in Chapter 10.

If an artist is pursuing multiple career ventures such as a combination of singing, acting, and songwriting, the manager needs to monitor the development of all of these talents objectively and decide with the artist how to present these talents. This may require going back to the previous stage of development. As an example, if an artist is highly developed as a performing artist but doesn't have a lot of recording experience, the demo may highlight a DVD or videotape and concert reviews along with the audio CD in order to show off the artist's immediate strengths. If highlighting your skills as a songwriter is a major consideration in the kind of deal you and your manager are seeking, it would be a good idea to have more originals than cover songs on the demo.

In my experience, the expense of creating the package sometimes becomes a major strain in the artist-manager relationship. I've seen a wide range of opinions on this touchy subject. On one hand, a number of artists and managers feel that it is part of the manager's responsibility to bankroll the demo package. On the other hand, some feel that the financial responsibility rests solely on the artist. Whatever the result may be to the issue of who pays for the demo package, it is the manager's responsibility to take the resources available to the artist—including such things as available cash, credit, studio, photographer, and musician relationships—and assist the artist in making the right relationships and deals that result in a package that can get an artist's point across effectively. This may require negotiating deferred payments or speculation deals, pulling in favors, and emotionally supporting the artist to take more time or curtail his other spending in order to invest in his own project. Any agreements made in connection with the development of demos should include who is responsible for any payment, what the amounts of any payment may be, when the payments are due (including very specific "triggering events" for speculation agreements, what credits are to be included on any demos, and what the limits of the performances or services on the demos may be used for. In addition, if the manager loans the artist money toward developing the package or invests any money into the artist's package and expects to get the investment back above and beyond the eventual commissions, the parties must map out a clear agreement of their understanding.

Industry Promotion

Demo package in hand, the manager moves on to their next responsibility: selling, or *shopping,* you to the industry and finding the opportunity that hopefully results in your break into the entertainment industry. To help in the shopping process, the manager may enlist the aid of other industry professionals, including entertainment lawyers, agents, and industry executives, who can assist in keeping the momentum of this shopping period going and, with any luck, getting a quick result. These third parties usually work for a fee, which can either be a flat "finder's fee" if and when a contact should pan out or a percentage of artist advances or royalties. It is the duty of the manager together with the artist and the artist's lawyer to negotiate these fees, which is a huge responsibility for an inexperienced manager. On one hand, the manager has a vested interest in retaining as much income as possible for the artist in the form of advances and future artist royalties, which also results in a higher management commission. On the other hand, to get the desired deal for the artist, the manager may find it necessary to share the wealth with others. It is crucial that both artist and manager are very clear and candid about how the eventual pie is split up when making deals at this juncture.

During the shopping period, the artist should support the manager's efforts as much as possible. This means continuing talent development, gigging, organizing showcases at a moment's notice, making themselves available for networking events and meetings, and generally giving the manager something to talk to the industry about. The initial promotion phase should come to an end when the manager and artist close a deal that results in the artist's first major opportunity. This deal can take a variety of forms, including an exclusive record contract, a publishing agreement, a part in a major theatrical production, recording session opportunities, or an extended road gig.

I should note here that *industry* promotion is distinct from promotion of the artist to the *public*. The manager should develop and implement a plan for promotion to the public in tandem with their promotion of the artist to the industry. The manager's role is important in public promotion both before and after the "big break" comes. These days, grassroots opinions weigh heavily on whether or not the industry will be interested in making a long-term investment in an artist. Of course, once the artist is in the limelight (for example, when his records begin selling), a completely new and important phase of promotion kicks in: the selling of the artist's image and products to an even wider public. The manager needs to be very involved in this process and work closely with other professionals such as record label promotions people and publicists to market the artist effectively.

The initial promotion phase of the artist-manager relationship is often the key "deal point" in an artist-manager contract because the first major industry opportunity is an objective, identifiable, and crucial result that both parties want and need in order for them to move forward together. When drafting contracts, the parties may consider basing future options on having a third-party deal in place. In other words, if the manager can't deliver a record deal, publishing deal, or other major opportunity to the artist, then the parties no longer have any obligations to each other. To protect the interest of the manager, the parties should consider how to compensate the manager and how to give them the opportunity to stay involved in your career if they do all of the work leading up to a third-party deal but simply runs out of time before finalizing it. Here is a scenario that can tragically affect both artist and manager: Suppose that the manager has a mandatory "sign or leave" clause deadline in his contract with an artist. If that deadline is looming, the manager might advise the artist to take just any deal that comes along—no matter how bad the terms may be—simply to meet that signing deadline and preserve the management contract. Flexibility, communication, and fairness are key in determining how to handle this type of situation.

When this initial opportunity comes to fruition, is the manager's work over? Absolutely not. It's just beginning. After the initial opportunity comes, it is usually the duty of the manager to add the shared accomplishment to the artist's resume and start all over again, trying to create and shop for the next opportunity. If done correctly and according to a well-conceived plan, the long range planning, industry promotions, and implementation of a series of these opportunities add up to a successful career in the industry for both the artist and manager.

Expansion

Once an artist's anchor opportunity is established, the manager really must go to work at expanding the artist's earning power even further. I like to think of this expansion as taking place both vertically and horizontally.

By vertical expansion, I mean taking the anchor opportunity and maximizing the productivity for the artist. For example, if the artist is with a record label, the manager has to do the things necessary to make the artist a priority at the label. These could include working with the label promotions team, finding a booking agent and setting up tours, or getting press coverage above and beyond what the label's publicity team gets. This is a crucial period, for the more work the manager does for the label, the more the label will do for the artist.

Simultaneously, the manager should help the artist expand horizontally, developing other talents and thus opening up other career opportunities. Many recording or performing artists have moved horizontally to songwriting for other artists, producing, acting, writing books, starting independent record labels, or pursuing management opportunities in the industry. A variety of new options open up once the artist's foot is in the door. As with any other business, carefully planned diversification is a must when it comes to sustaining the artist's career.

During this phase of expansion of an artist's career, the manager—with the consent of the artist—usually assembles the rest of the management team. The team could include a lawyer, a publicist to handle press duties, an accountant, an agent, and other professionals. This is an important phase of the artist's growth and the manager needs to be able to shift into this delegation phase while coordinating the team and keeping the artist's career moving forward.

The Exit Plan

This last phase is one that, sadly, most artists and inexperienced managers forget to address. The ride ends. Time and time again, we see for ourselves or hear about an act well beyond its prime doing gigs or making one more try at a comeback, or living some obscure and financially strapped life, as the public asks, "Whatever happened to...?" These days, a recording artist's career is considered a success on a major label if they release five albums during their tenure with the label, along with accompanying concert tours.

For a manager and artist, that means a 7- to 10-year period of making money in the industry to balance the early, lean years of development, and being in the limelight needs to segue into a combination of financial and personal stability in order for the artist to exit the industry with some semblance of dignity and emotional stability. It means that once the flow of money begins, it is wise to consult a good accountant and financial advisor to plan for the future. If the artist sustains popularity and financial success well beyond the norm, then great, but the public is fickle and demands new stars on a regular basis, so an exit/retirement plan is very important for a manager and artist to develop.

Major Contract Points

With the foregoing overview of the artist-management relationship and its life span as a backdrop, let's take a look at some of the major points of discussion that are usually included in the negotiation of an artist management agreement. Of course, every individual and every relationship is different, so whether you are an artist considering a manager or visa versa, be sure to take the time to carefully review the Companion Questions at the end of the chapter to really get a clear picture of what you are willing to put into this relationship and what you expect to get out of this relationship. Both artist and manager are putting a great deal of trust in each other to move forward together in a highly speculative business; the decisions made for each and all of these individual components can be positively or negatively long-lasting for both parties.

Establishment of the Artist-Manager Relationship

Regardless of the prior relationship of the artist and manager, the first thing that a management agreement should do is clearly state the desire of the parties to establish a formal artist-manager relationship. An agreement may include a preamble stating what each party will bring to the relationship by listing the expertise, skills, and talents of the parties followed by a statement that the manager will be charged with the obligation to manage the artist's career.

However this opening statement is phrased, it is meant to eliminate any misunderstandings with respect to the relationship between the parties. As the hypothetical at the beginning of this chapter illustrated, there are a number of variations of relationships ranging from being a friend to an advisor-teacher that all can be interpreted as being a management or pseudo-management relationship. A formal, preferably written agreement between an artist with that artist's intended manager removes all speculation of who is the manager—especially for any other party who feels that they may be the artist's manager.

Length of Agreement

A management agreement may last a short period; it may last forever. The term of the artist-management relationship is absolutely negotiable. It can be for a set period (for example, five years) with a definitive start and end date. A variation on a set period of time that gives the parties some flexibility is to have a set period (for example, one year) with a series of options (three one-year options for a total of four years) that need to be exercised by one party or the other. The options could be tied to performance such as established professional goals or to specified earning plateaus for the artist. Using these benchmarks as guide, if the artist-manager relationship does not result in the artist being able to meet the professional or financial expectations of the parties, they can terminate the agreement at the end of a period cleanly.

The length of an artist-manager agreement can be "at will," meaning that it will run perpetually until one of the parties gives the other notice that they would like to terminate the agreement. Another variation is for the term of the agreement to be project-based, identifying a so-called "cycle" in an artist's career that the manager will be involved in. For example, if a management agreement is based on a two album production and sales cycle, the starting point would include the inception of the A&R and creative aspects of the recording of the first album and then extend through all of the sales/promotions efforts—including touring—of the second album. This way, the manager can be involved in nurturing all aspects of the artist's career associated with the cycle, coordinating the team involved with the artist over the period of time necessary to bring these projects to full fruition, and reap the rewards of their labor from the projects they are directly hired to manage.

When discussing the length of a management agreement, the parties must take great care in realistically determining how much ramp-up time will be required to get an artist ready to earn money from their talents, what is a fair amount of time to form the tools necessary to create opportunities, and to actually exploit those opportunities. Conversely, it is important for a management agreement to be short enough to make sure that the manager has the incentive to put the artist in a position to earn a living while not compromising the integrity of the artist's talents or launching the artist prematurely.

Duties and Obligations

The agreement should include realistic and objective duties for the manager to be responsible for. It is essentially a job description, enumerating roles such as representing the artist to the industry; advising and consulting the artist in matters like presentation, material, and personnel; assembling a team of professionals for the artist; and being the overall coordinator of the artist's career.

If there are objective and specific benchmarks or duties that are very particular to how you want to be managed, this is a good opportunity to spell those out as specific duties. For example, because of the unique working relationship you have developed with you manager leading up to the formalizing of your agreement, if a primary duty of the manager is to coordinate your live performances and/or touring rather than delegate those duties to an outside tour manager, that duty could be included in this section of your agreement.

Some managers use this as an opportunity to make it clear what they are *not* going to do for an artist. Managers are not booking agents, publicists, publishers, or record labels. In today's "Do-It-Yourself" artist business model, sometimes the expectation of what a manager's duties are can be overwhelming. There is a huge difference between a manager interfacing with a third-party record label and actually running one because an artist decided it's the best way to get their own music out to the public. Clarity is the key for both parties; to avoid any misunderstanding of the manager's duties, try to spell them out. That way, if you have any issues with performance or non-performance of the manager's obligations, you have a document you can refer to that spells out what your mutual expectations were. Talk these through thoroughly with each other so you know clearly what is and will be expected in the relationship.

Limits of Authority—Powers of Attorney

To balance out the duties of the manager, it's wise to spell out specifically what the manager is not authorized to do. An attitude and policy of an artist putting their head in the sand, telling the world "my manager's handling it," and then hoping for the best is not a good idea. There are certain actions that an artist has to take full responsibility for and one of the best ways to do it is to reserve those rights rather than allow a manager to do them for you. Negotiating checks, signing documents on an artist's behalf, making creative decisions, handling money, making investments, taking care of non-entertainment matters—these are all actions that could potentially be disastrous when placed in the hands of the wrong person—manager included.

Of particular note are the instances above where the manager is signing documents or acting on behalf of a client. This is called a power of attorney and should be reviewed closely when deciding if a manager should be given such broad and important rights. If a power of attorney is granted to a manager, it is advisable to do so with limitations on the scope of such power of attorney. Things like being able to negotiate and cash checks, obligate an artist financially, or sign long-term contracts are usually reserved for the artist and not included in any power of attorney.

Commission and Expenses

The results of your discussion of how much to pay the manager and how to pay them are based on the factors addressed earlier in this chapter and are incorporated into your agreement. In addition, the payment by a manager of expenses related to the artist's career and reimbursement of those expenses by the artist should be included in the document. Some considerations include limitations of expenses, either in terms of dollar figures or of types of expenses. For example, it is common for management agreements to require that a manager obtain authority from an artist to spend more than $200 at one time on behalf of a client. A variation could be for the artist to be responsible for coach airfare if a manager is traveling on behalf of the client; if the manager decides to fly business class, the artist would only be responsible for the coach fare; the manager is responsible for the upgrade cost.

Determining the periodic time for payment and expense reimbursement to a manager is also advisable. Will the manager be paid within 30 days of the receipt of any earnings by the artist, or will it be monthly or quarterly? Does the manager have to present the artist with an invoice and receipts for reimbursement? All of the so-called "money issues" should be clearly spelled out so the parties themselves and any third parties hired by the parties (such as accountants and business managers) could act accordingly.

Exclusivity

Usually, a manager will request that she be the only person advising the artist. This is for purposes of having continuity in the implementation of a career plan, not confusing third parties by having too many cooks in the kitchen, and to avoid the payment of multiple managers. Too often, this provision is treated as a manager's effort to smother an artist and cut them off from the rest of the industry's professional world. It is a good policy to discuss the extent of the "comfort zone" that a manager has with the artist having additional advisors and teachers to bounce ideas off of. Like any very private and trusting relationship, jealousy and suspicion can develop when a manager or artist feels that the relationship is being breached by bringing in additional advisors.

At the same time, most experienced managers retain the right to provide their management services for other artists. Parties should be candid about whether or not the manager is potentially spread too thin when taking on other artists. An agreement may include a requirement of how much attention should be given to the client, put limits on numbers of management clients a manager may have, or a provision requiring that the manager remains available throughout the term of the agreement as the primary person (instead of a partner, employee, or intern) responsible for the artist's career.

These are just a few of the terms that are included in a typical artist-manager relationship. It has been stated over the years that the artist-manager relationship is much like a marriage. Some have withstood tests of time that have lasted decades, and weathered severe storms of the ups and downs of the business. One of the likely reasons that these relationships last so long is that the agreements made between the parties are usually fair, and they addressed issues with care, candor, trust, periodic review, and flexibility. If you find the right combination in a manager or management team that can bridge your business and art into a sustained career, the agreement you craft should be one that reflects your trust and shared vision.

Companion Questions

1. *How did you come in contact with the person whom you are considering to manage you? Was it a referral? Who introduced you to each other?*

2. *Do you communicate clearly with each other? Do you share the bad news as well as the good news with each other?*

3. *Have you developed a clear plan of action together? Do you have common goals, ambitions, and personal and career objectives? How do these interface with each other?*

4. *How long are you willing to commit to an artist-management relationship? Do you want your relationship to be "at will" or for a set period of time?*

5. *Do you represent each other professionally and with dignity in the business?*

6. *What are the limits of the manager's authority to represent you?*

7. *How much should the manager be compensated? On what should you base the commission?*

8. *Is the manager expected to invest money in you as an artist?*

9. *Do the parties have any other kind of business relationship (for example, producer/artist or label/artist)?*

10. *Do you have concrete professional goals that you are trying to achieve individually and together?*

11. *Are you learning and growing in the business together at the same pace? If not, why not? Do you share information and your contacts with each other?*

12. *Are you willing to have a personal as well as professional relationship with each other? If you are a manager, how involved do you want to get in your artist's personal life? If you are an artist, how much do you want your manager to be involved in your personal life? Do you know how to say "no" to each other?*

6 Performance Agreements

Ask music fans to name their most memorable live shows and they are likely to drift off to a magic place as they recall a piece of their lives surrounded by music, other people, and a musician on stage who was the center of their memory. Ask musicians the same question and they are likely to give you a similar answer, only from the point of view of the stage. Musicians' live performances are a unique opportunity for them to create a special bond with an audience that could last a lifetime. This special relationship is the basis of the live music business, complete with its own cast of participants and unique twists in the law.

The basic components that make up the live music business are relatively simple and have been with us for as long as audiences have been willing to lay out their hard-earned dollars to be entertained. When you think about it, the throngs who gathered at the Coliseum in ancient Rome to watch a re-creation of an epic battle were not much different from a modern-day concert audience. A person putting together a show—be it a concert promoter, a television show producer, or the night-club owner down the street—knows of an audience that is in need of entertainment and is willing to pay money for that entertainment. The presenter can gather this audience together with the right combination of time, location, setting, price point, and talent.

There are many variations on the basic promoter-talent-audience triangle just described, but from a string quartet playing a wedding at a church to a band on a 40-city tour with a fleet of buses and semis hauling personnel, stage rigging, and gear, most of the legal issues remain the same. In this chapter, we will briefly look at some of these issues and how they are incorporated into agreements for personal appearances.

Hypothetical: A Tour de Farce

The Beats Being Dead Band, also known as BBDB, a four-piece rock band, has built up a strong regional following over the years. BBDB can bring in audiences of several hundred people at a time when headlining at clubs and has occasionally opened up for major label acts in arena-type venues. BBDB makes a significant amount of its income from selling its recordings, autographed posters, T-shirts, and other merchandise when gigging.

A promoter asked whether BBDB was interested in a 15-week tour opening for two major label acts. The promoter explained that the band would have to provide its own gear and transportation because the tour bus was already packed, but a weekly fee and per diems would be taken care of as well as the hotel rooms along the way. BBDB jumped at that chance and accepted the tour.

In an effort to make a good impression with the major acts, BBDB decided to "beef up" its act, adding two more musicians and three dancers to give their show a more unique stage presence. BBDB agreed to pay these additional members a weekly fee to join the tour. The band members also invited half a dozen friends of theirs to come along as their road crew and to pose as the band's entourage in exchange for food and gas money and the opportunity to party with some major stars. The friends couldn't wait to join this rock and roll vacation.

BBDB enjoyed a great deal of newfound success as a touring band. The band especially became known to the audience and the press for the wild stage show and the "BBDB Party Posse" that became one of the trademarks of the tour. A live concert DVD was made of one of the shows featuring the backstage antics of everyone involved with the band. One of the songs from the DVD was aired on a popular website and it became one of the most watched videos for weeks, bringing much attention to the band and the tour. Egos began to swell along with their success. Four weeks into the tour, the friends who were in the entourage realized that they were identified as integral parts of the show and demanded to have extra backstage passes and their own dressing room for the rest of the tour. They also demanded more "extras" on their rider to make up for the lack of pay.

Ten weeks into the tour, a major label executive approached the original members of BBDB after a show with an offer to sign the entire "BBDB and the Party Posse" to an exclusive artist multimedia deal including audio and live concert recordings. They threw a party to celebrate the offer. The Party Posse unfortunately lived up to its name. An argument broke out when the original members of BBDB broke the news to everyone that they were not going to be included in the deal as part of the act. The dancers threatened to block the use of the existing DVD in any way if they were not paid "big money" to be included on the product. Members of the BBDB entourage trashed their hotel rooms and the lobby restaurant, throwing all of the band's instruments into a bonfire in the parking lot to in an effort to show that they can "rock with the best of them." One member, while intoxicated, physically and verbally assaulted the label executive. The executive not only revoked the offer to the band, but threatened to sue them and warn the rest of the industry about their "crazy behavior."

Scope of Performance

Both parties to a performance contract should be very clear about what services the talent is expected to render—sometimes called the scope of the performance. These parameters help the performer develop a sense of how much preparation the performance will take, what kind of equipment and personnel will be needed, how much time will have to be set aside for the performance—all of which factor into how to set the fee for the performance. For example, if you are putting together musicians to play a gig, are the musicians expected to get together for a certain number of rehearsals? If you will be headlining at a major concert, are you expected to appear at press conferences and radio shows to promote the show? If you are playing at a wedding, is your string quartet expected to play at the ceremony and the reception? Does appearing on stage obligate you to do the backstage "meet and greet" autograph sessions? The parties should discuss and arrange all of these details when exploring the scope of the performance.

A performance agreement may also restrict the performer from certain activities. For example, a promoter may wish to restrict you from performing within a certain geographical distance for a period of time. In another instance, a television show producer may ask that you refrain from appearing on a similar and competing television show. By limiting an audience's opportunity to see you, the promoter increases the value of the ticket. Side musicians are sometimes exclusively hired, resulting in being restricted from taking certain other gigs for the duration of a tour or for a series of performances. Other times, musicians are hired on a "first-call" basis, which—while non-exclusive—allows the hiring party priority over other potential parties when using the musician's services.

Where and When?

Probably the two most important details of any live performance are where and when your services as a performer are needed. This is directly tied into the scope of your performance. It is extremely important to document details such as locations of stages, specific rooms within a large venue, pick-up locations, and promotion appearance addresses. Details such as stage times, sound checks, rehearsals, and promotional stops all become part of the time element of performance agreements. One crucial detail for acts that travel extensively is to factor in the differences in time and date zones. Showing up on the wrong day for a gig because you had a 12-hour flight and forgot to factor in the change from a.m. to p.m. can be embarrassing and open you up to legal liability.

Passing the Hat

From a club gig for all the beer you can drink to a world tour, a major issue for every performer is how much and how to get paid. Pay scales for performers vary widely, but the basic issues involved are relatively easy to grasp.

One way to get paid is to have a *guarantee*. As with any other service, the two parties agree upon a set fee for the services rendered. This fee can be based on the entire appearance, on an hourly rate, on a series of performances, or on a variety of other configurations. What is key in this type of payment arrangement is to state clearly the basis and limits of the services to be rendered for the amount of money to be paid. Your scope of service, discussed previously, is important when determining whether any extra money is due to you if you provide services above and beyond the terms of your agreement. If you are hired to perform for three hours at a private party and the party-goers are having a great time, it is not out of line for you to ask for additional pay to perform another set or two beyond the time you were hired to perform.

A second form of payment is the *contingent payment,* which is a payment based on money that is not guaranteed, but rather, derived from speculative source. This can be based on ticket sales, amount of money from the bar, donations, or other types of income. The concept of "a piece of the gate receipts" can either be a blessing or a curse, depending on how well a show is promoted, the draw of the acts involved, or unforeseen circumstances that affect attendance.

Often, promoters and performers will agree to combine the guarantee and contingency fees. In this arrangement, the promoter will guarantee a minimum amount for a performance and then include an additional *back-end* fee based on the contingency. For example, a club could guarantee a fee of $500 with a contingency of 50 percent of all ticket sales above $1,000. If the tickets are $10 apiece and 150 people attend the show, the artist receives the $500 guarantee plus an additional $250, which is 50 percent of the $500 taken in by the club above the first 100 people to buy tickets. In this case, the parties are sharing the risks of the live performance. Venues are under the scrutiny of federal and state taxation authorities, so they have a duty to report earnings of musicians. Any payments made directly to a performer are clearly considered taxable income, but some payments made to performers as reimbursements for costs that they incurred might not be considered taxable. When structuring more sophisticated payment arrangements, it is a good practice to speak to a tax advisor to help you.

Other payment issues include whether a deposit or advance is required to secure a date; what, if any, extra payments are to be made by the promoter on your behalf; whether merchandise income becomes part of a fee; and what the consequences of a "no-show" are. In addition, the more sophisticated a performance becomes, the more opportunity there is to generate more income, requiring more detail in the financial issues involved in the business dealings. Deductions from the gross receipts—including such items as PRO payments, union fees, venue participation in merchandise sales, fees paid to support acts, promotional costs, and other costs—can affect the eventual performance fee dramatically.

Travel and Accommodations

Getting to and from the venue, sleeping, and eating are also important details to consider. For acts playing in local venues, these discussions may include preferential parking in a club's parking lot for load-in and convenience and getting a free dinner between sets. Other times, discussions will center on airfare, ground transportation, arrangements for hotels, cash allowances for meals, and other personal costs (known as *per diems*) while you are involved in the engagement. Although you do not want to turn yourself into a travel agent, you might want to start thinking like one. Traveling on the right off-peak day and adding a night in a hotel may be just the thing that affects the total price of the package you are offering to a promoter and closes a deal. Think twice about trying to squeeze in connections that are far too close or about the financial impact of missing a plane and having to change a ticket purchased a month in advance to one purchased an hour before travel. A tour manager once shared a horror story with me about a person on a tour who slept in on three occasions, missing three flights that were crossing the Atlantic Ocean, resulting in thousands of dollars in extra airfare alone! Check-in times are also an important issue. Sometimes in an effort to save money, the promoter will request that you check into a hotel only after a performance to avoid paying the extra charges. However, if you need to rest or simply gather your thoughts before a performance, both you and the promoter, as well as the audience, will ultimately be happier because of the additional consideration given to your working conditions.

Contract Riders

A contract rider is a crucial component of the performance agreement spelling out the specific, unique, and particular requirements that a promoter must provide to a performer in order to secure their services. If there is one thing that the entire music industry has to thank the 1970s for, it is the wild and crazy performance riders that were made famous by the characters playing big-time rock concerts. Demands that included vast amounts of alcohol and drugs, particular colors of candy, and just about any vice imaginable have reached legendary status in music law circles. While your own rider may one day be considered one of the classics, even at a modest level, it is an important part of your appearance agreement.

The first part of your rider is the *technical rider*. Many artists' shows have been reduced to mediocrity due to the ever-present "technical difficulty," leaving parties at odds with each other over fault. Fortunately, much of this difficulty can be avoided with some planning, discussion, and mutual agreement. Venue and facility requirements are a good starting point. A 13-piece band might not fit on the 8-by-12-foot stage. Separate dressing rooms for males and females may be in order. Parking closer than six blocks away would be nice. It all adds up to an understanding of what is an acceptable venue. Second on the technical rider are issues such as electrical, sound and light, instrument, equipment, and any special effects requirements. A single electrical circuit supporting four bands' worth of gear is likely to blow out. A singer may want to bring her own makeup and hair personnel because the show is going to be broadcast worldwide. A piano duo I represented kept running into roadblocks because some towns in the United States don't have two matching grand pianos within their city limits. This list can go on and on depending on the artist, but your act is the one that counts. Carefully review your minimum technical requirements and your ideal technical requirements and put them in writing for others to see and use. You and your audience will be thankful later.

The second part is what I call your "comfort and courtesy" rider points, some of which are considered necessities, others extravagances, depending on whom you talk to. Issues such as catering, what gets you "in the mood" to perform, who is included on your guest list, and all of the variations that you can come up with to outdo the 1970s riders are part of this section of your rider. Consider what is truly necessary for you to perform, what makes things convenient for you, and whether your requests are ego-driven instead of performance-driven. As with other terms of a live performance agreement, whether or not you can successfully negotiate your technical or comfort and courtesy rider is largely a result of relative bargaining position. Whether or not your requirements are characterized as reasonable or outrageous is directly tied in to how badly a promoter wants you to perform.

Liability to Your Audience

The promoter and performer both owe a duty to their audience to put on a show that will not harm those in attendance. Tragedies such as fires, audience members being trampled due to general admission seating, and injuries sustained from being struck by objects flung from the stage (including pieces of musical instruments, promotional items, and the musicians themselves) or throughout the crowd are often attributed to the performing musicians. In recent years, audience members and their lawyers have broadened the scope of this "basic safety" notion in an attempt to find musicians liable for actions on the stage that resulted in emotional distress or personal injury, and even for breaching an implied product warranty by putting on a subpar show that wasn't worth the ticket price.

Above and beyond the potential civil liabilities to consider, there are also possible criminal issues associated with performing live and being on tour. "Entertaining" by getting into fights with audience members or security personnel may lead to criminal charges to the performer. Depending on the city or state, certain actions on stage may be considered obscene, thus punishable by authorities. Another potential civil liability for performer to consider is that of sexual harassment. Be it on the stage or off, sexual harassment may not be tolerated as part of the musician lifestyle as much as it has been in the past. Accordingly, although rare, there are touring acts that are popular precisely because they are offensive, harassing, and obscene. Nevertheless, excessive and unjustified violence against another human being is still considered criminal in all municipalities.

Many artists are unpleasantly surprised when they become legally responsible for the actions of their support staff, crew, and hangers-on. Under theories of stretching liability to reach into the deepest pockets, arguments are regularly made that the artists themselves or the artists' record labels are financially responsible for the misdeeds of individuals who are even remotely related to the artist. Time and time again, record labels end up paying settlements to people who have been injured by a person who is either officially or unofficially tied to an artist. In these cases, the artist can eventually become responsible for the repayment of these settlements to the label out of future royalties.

We could, at this point, launch into a theoretical discussion of the First Amendment, the value of "street credibility" to your resume, or the validity of what some would consider frivolous claims against artists and how they might affect your free expression. The extreme of these cases resulting in lawsuits against an artist and its label for injuries alleged to have been caused as a result of "listening to the band's records." I'll leave that for you to take on at a more appropriate time and place. However, you should be aware that your legal duty and potential liability to your audience has become vastly expanded beyond simply putting on a good show and hoping that they go away singing your songs.

No-Show Penalties

If an artist doesn't or can't make a performance, the solution might not be as simple as waiving the fee that was to be paid. If a promoter has spent money in anticipation of your appearance and was due to make a profit from the show, he may be entitled to costs related to your not following through on your end of the bargain. In cases where ticket sales have to be refunded to would-be attendees, the penalties can run very high, both in terms of your finances and reputation.

Contractually, most performance agreements should have a contingency plan for circumstances beyond your control. Commonly referred to "force majeur" or "acts of God," parties on both sides of a performance contract usually agree not to hold each other responsible for things that neither party anticipated and could not have avoided. Occurrences such as natural disasters (earthquakes, tornadoes), acts of civil disobedience or crime (riots, so-called "acts of terror"), or labor disputes (strikes that result in venues being closed or cancellation of television shows) are often considered "force majeur" occurrences. Clearly, in emergency situations, rescheduling a performance could be a solution. However, in cases where the date can't change (for example, a wedding engagement or an awards show for television that cannot be rescheduled), your help in mitigating the promoter's damages will go a long way toward lessening your financial liability and saving your reputation. Mitigating actions on your part could include notification as soon as possible that you can't perform and suggesting or finding a replacement act.

Merchandising

Ticket sales are no longer the only source of income when it comes to the performing musician. The sale of merchandise has become a major component of the music industry. You need to consider a variety of legal issues when setting up merchandising deals.

One of the first details that you need to take care of when considering merchandise is the ownership of the trademarks and copyrights being used on items that you intend to sell. Logos, artwork, and even tour names (for example, "The Crazy Cowboys on Rampage Tour") are trademarks that must be protected to ensure that only authorized merchandise is being manufactured and sold. If you hire a graphic designer to create a visual rendition of your act's or tour's trademark, be sure that your agreement with the artist includes clear language about the ownership of trademarks and copyrights. It would be unfortunate if you hired an artist to design your CD cover and were surprised when they demanded extra payment from you because the money you originally paid to create the cover didn't include the right to put the image on all of the posters and T-shirts you are selling at gigs. Worse yet, the designer may demand that you destroy all of the "unauthorized" merchandise that you created without their permission.

If you are handling all of the details of manufacturing your merchandise, you will need to contract with the various vendors doing the work for you. Manufacturing agreements include details such as delivery dates, quality control, who is financially responsible for shipping the items, what to do about delays, and a wide variety of other matters related to the manufacturing process. Depending on how far into the process you get (remembering that some major rock acts make more money from merchandise than they do from record sales or ticket sales), you may consider setting up a completely separate entity for your business just to handle the merchandise matters. You and your legal team should become well versed in the Uniform Commercial Code (UCC), a body of law that legislates the buying and selling of goods in the marketplace.

Once you have your merchandise in hand, you need to negotiate with venues regarding whether you can sell merchandise at all when you play a gig and, if so, what your revenue split is going to be between the band and the venue. Obtaining licenses, taking care of proper accounting, and payment of the appropriate taxes are also issues that may arise when you sell your wares along with your music.

If you have reached a level of popularity with your audience that makes your merchandise a valuable asset, a third party may want to enter into an exclusive merchandise agreement with you. Much like an exclusive artist deal, these are potentially lucrative agreements in which you receive royalties based on revenue generated from the items sold bearing your name, likeness, and trademarks. Length of the exclusivity, what items are included in the deal, advances, and royalty rates are all major negotiating points of merchandise agreements.

Ancillary Audio Visual Products

A new technological twist has entered into the merchandise field with more and more acts selling self-produced audiovisual merchandise like concert footage or "behind the scenes" videos and DVDs. The posting and broadcasting of video footage on the Internet needs to be considered by artists as well. Interesting legal issues arise as to whether or not these types of items are included in the record company's exclusive artist agreements or what songs can or can't be included on a set list based on whether or not permission will be granted to include them on an item that will be offered for sale. You should also consider the "name and likeness" clearances required from anyone and anything that will potentially appear on camera, including the fans attending your concerts.

Parties to performance agreements also should consider if and how broadcasts and recordings of their performances factor into the agreement. Adding broadcasts and recordings to the scope of performance may result in an additional audience and additional products that may require additional compensation. Note that there's a difference between archive recordings for the purposes of keeping a record of an event and revenue-generating commercial recordings. If a performance will be broadcast, distributed, given away, or sold, then additional rights, including the rights to use the songs, biographical materials, and a performer's likeness may have to be secured. Allowing a club to videotape your performance of an original song so they can show it in-house is very different from the club's selling the same performance to a production company for television broadcast and inclusion on a DVD for public sale.

As you can see, the merchandising field can take on a life of its own. It would be wise to assess whether your "merchandisability" could be a lucrative adjunct to your musicianship. Many lawyers specialize in merchandise and licensing law, protecting the images and legal interests of those artists whose names and trademarks can be monetized into merchandisable goods.

Personnel

Finally, when dealing with your performance agreements, you need to address the various people required to get you on stage. If you are truly a "one man band" handling every artistic and business aspect of your performances, none of the following discussion will apply to you; however, most professional musicians will at one time or another have to consider some of these issues.

Side Musicians

When working with side musicians, it is crucial to make clear that you are hiring them for particular services and that they are not permanent members of your band. If these details aren't clear, serious problems can arise if your act reaches a notable level of success and the side musicians are expecting to move along with you to the next phase of your career. If you are not a principal member of an act, you are considered a side musician. Side musicians usually are independent contractors or "hired guns" who support the act on a limited basis. Be sure to clarify your status at the outset of a project to avoid any bad feelings or, worse, litigation down the road.

Side musician agreements deal with the basic time, place, scope, and price details discussed earlier in this chapter, except that the contracting party is the principal act instead of a promoter. Side musicians usually negotiate a set fee for their time. This can be based on a per-gig basis, a daily basis, weekly basis, or "entire run" basis if the act is touring. Because side musicians work on a freelance basis and need to pick up work where and when they can find it, if an act wants to have "first call" or priority on a side musician's scheduling, a retainer fee is sometimes negotiated, guaranteeing the side musician extra money whether or not the act has a gig.

Lodging, transportation, and per diem rates are also issues when it comes to side musicians. Often, the principal acts will stay at nicer hotels and travel by a completely separate mode of travel (say, by airplane instead of bus) or in separate classes.

The duties of the side musicians should also be taken into consideration. Do the side musicians get paid for rehearsals? Do they have to participate in "meet and greets" backstage, attend promotional events, or sign autographs along with the band? Are they required to allow the use of their names and likenesses for promotional or merchandising purposes? What if the principals decide to sell recordings of concerts? Is there an extra fee involved or is it considered part of the "live performance"?

Finally, issues such as protection of the side musicians' health, equipment, and reputation can arise. If you talk to enough side musicians, you will hear horror story after horror story about what can happen to them while supporting an act on the road. From knee injuries sustained on stage due to the show's choreography to being arrested for being in the wrong place at the wrong time when a band is out "just having some fun," who is legally responsible for what happens to a side musician is a major contract point of any side musician agreement.

Agents

Hiring a booking agent to help you secure gigs can be one of the biggest decisions of your career. While they are a part of an artist's management team, the agent is not a manager. An agent's sole purpose is to procure employment for you. The manager's role is to develop the larger, overall business plan for you.

Negotiating the terms and conditions of an agent's agreement is very important. This person has a limited, but very specific, role, and his or her effectiveness can make or break your career. Again, the big three issues of scope, time, and money are key when you decide on an agent.

Some agents require you to enter into exclusive agreements with them, which avoids duplication of effort and the question of which agent is deserving of a commission. Before entering into an exclusive agreement, however, consider the scope of the exclusivity. Is the agent a "full service" agent or does the agent specialize in only specific forms of entertainment? For example, does the agent deal only with concert performances and not television? If you are also an actor, does the agent have access to theater or movie roles? You may wish to consider limiting the scope of the agency based on the capabilities of the agent. You may also want to test drive the relationship prior to considering exclusivity.

If you decide to enter into an exclusive relationship with an agent, the next issue is the length of the relationship. Some artists stay with agencies for years, the two of them working hand in hand to grow into successful enterprises together. Other artists plan their growth by working with a smaller agency to get their career started and then moving on to a larger one as their careers take off. Negotiating the length of the agency agreement, then, becomes tricky because while the artist wants to maximize the income from the time spent with the agent, the agent may be reluctant to devote time and effort into an artist if the artist is not willing to let the agent reap the benefits of sending her into the big leagues.

As with the manager, the amount of an agent's commission and the basis of this commission are negotiable issues. Be sure to consider whether a commissionable item is one that goes immediately to your hard costs. For example, if your travel or hotel rooms are paid for or reimbursed by a promoter, should an agent be able to commission that "extra" amount? How about money that you make from the sale of merchandise or from ancillary income not earned from the engagement? A final issue to consider with an agent is whether the agent will be paid for establishing your relationship with a venue, even if you are no longer working with that particular agent.

As always, the effectiveness of working with your agent is largely based on the development of a solid relationship. The legal issues that arise are largely a result of how well this relationship is established, documented, and carried out.

Other Personnel

The larger an act gets, the more complex and complicated the legal issues regarding personnel issues can be. Other live performance personnel to consider include people involved with tour management services, technical services, transportation, hair and makeup, accounting services, security, all the way through to personal chefs and massage therapists. The hiring, firing, and management of all of these people require legal review every step of the way.

The one-on-one live performance is still the most lasting relationship that many artists can develop with their audience. While the legal issues have become more complex with the addition of technology, cross-marketing, and the relationship with other aspects of an artist's career, they are manageable with the proper amount of planning and attention to detail.

Promoters as the "New" Major Labels

A recent development in the music industry has been the signing of major label acts who haven't proven themselves to be a "hot ticket" to multimillion-dollar, multiyear, exclusive arrangements with concert promotions companies. While the standards of these deals are unfolding in real time, they appear to be the "new" equivalent to major label recording agreements. Artists who have proven success as live acts can secure their financial stability by agreeing to exclusive arrangements with one company to present their live shows for a number of years for an advance in appearance fees. Lucrative sources of income such as merchandise, broadcasts, Internet-based income, and live performance videos are all shared between the artist and the promoters and require expert negotiation of each term of ownership and shared income, much like the traditional record deal.

With these types of arrangements, the basic low-tech talent of putting on a great performance has been married to the new high-tech world of instantaneous distribution of these performances. By securing the major fees for their performances up front, artists no longer have to rely on advances from record labels secured by having to produce future recordings. This could potentially lead to a more independent and thus creative approach to recording new music by the artists who enter into these types of deals.

The live performance has come full circle in the cycle of the entertainment industry. As I emphasized from the outset of this chapter, the artist who can connect with an audience and deliver the great performance has the opportunity to make a lasting impression that can be experienced over and over again and will hopefully pay the performer over and over, thanks to the technology and new business model that is emerging for live performers.

Companion Questions

1. *Do you perform live to support your recordings or do you record to support your live performances?*

2. *What are the key elements of your live performance? What are the "extras," meaning those elements you can do without?*

3. *Do you have specific technical requirements for your live performances? Can they be put in writing and/or a diagram for others to follow easily?*

4. *If you are a recording artist or a production company that has different personnel from your live performance team, should you form a separate business entity for each?*

5. *When quoting a talent fee to someone who wants to hire you, does it include all of the ancillary costs of your performance? Do you make these costs clear to the promoter or artist hiring you?*

6. *How are you to be paid? Is there a deposit? Is there an agent? How do you calculate any back-end payments? Can you monitor how these payments are calculated?*

7. *Is there an identifiable audience demographic that you attract to your shows? Can you think of a non-music-related company that would be interested in sponsoring you in order to reach your audience?*

8. *Do you record your shows? Do you use these recordings for demo and promotional purposes? Do you include these recordings as a products that you sell or allow others to sell? Do you post these recordings on websites or allow others to do so?*

9. *Have you secured all of the rights for your promotional materials? For your merchandise?*

10. *Is your live performance potentially dangerous or offensive to your audience?*

11. *When hiring musicians and other personnel, do you factor in that you may be ultimately responsible to third parties for their behavior patterns or actions?*

Business As Usual

7 Business Entities

O ne of the messiest events a musician can ever participate in is
the good old-fashioned band fight. A band fight could stem
from relatively tame issues such as "artistic differences" that
arise just before the band hits the stage, which results in musicians that
glare at each other while performing, stalk off after getting their share
of the gig's earnings, and stop speaking to their bandmates for weeks.
The band fight can even get physical over business differences—a fist
fight once broke out at my desk and spilled out onto the street below
when a lead singer confessed to his band mates that his career plan was
to dump them as soon as they hit the big time. Sadly, fans sometimes
become spectators when a major label act with years of earnings
behind them breaks up, resulting in disagreements over who is entitled
to a share in future royalties. It can turn what started out as a band
made up of the best of friends into courtroom combatants fighting
over their hard-earned millions with the aid of litigation lawyers.

All variations of the band fight are reminders that the type of entity
you establish for conducting business is an extremely important decision for you to make in your musical career. Your choice of business
entity will affect a variety of important issues, including who you will
be surrounded by on a regular basis, how you make business decisions,
and how large your slice of the profit pie will be. In this chapter, I will
introduce you to the common entities that musicians use for conducting business. Regardless of your reasons for considering a business
entity, it's a good idea to weigh the advantages and disadvantages of
each before making a decision.

Hypothetical Situation: Strange Bedfellows

Derek, a drummer, and Geri, a guitarist, were an inseparable team. They started playing music together in junior high jazz band and never stopped. As they developed together in talent and friendship, they worked as a rhythm team for a number of musical groups in a variety of musical styles. As bands came and went, these two continued to work together. Eventually, Derek and Geri developed their vocal skills, composed music together, and opened a small music production studio together. When Derek and Geri opened their studio, DG Music Productions in their early 20s, they pooled their resources, each bringing the equipment they had amassed over the years. They also each contributed $3,000 apiece to the business and took out a loan at a bank together for the business. DG Music Productions did not have a formal partnership agreement.

Sara, a vocalist, was recording a demo at DG Music Productions backed up by her younger brother Bobby and her boyfriend, Francois. Bobby and Francois were not very good musicians, but they were supportive of Sara's career goals and never asked for money for backing her up in the small clubs where she performed. Derek and Geri both really liked Sara's voice and drive, so when she asked if she, Bobby, and Francois could record at the studio for free with "no strings attached" for six months, Derek and Geri gave it their green light. She developed her artistic skills over time at DGMP while Bobby and Francois spent most of their time hanging out and making and impressing new friends by bringing them to "the band's" studio.

Not liking how slow things were moving for Sara and believing she was getting nowhere with Bobby and Francois, Derek and Geri asked Sara if she would be willing to let them get artistically involved in her project. Sara jumped at the chance and immediately started to write with the two of them as well as use them as the primary musicians on her recordings. Sara wanted to keep the peace with Bobby and Francois and motivate them to work harder on their music, so she requested that Derek and Geri "do her a favor" and allow her brother and boyfriend to play on her tracks, knowing that their subpar musicianship would not make it to the final mixes of the recordings. Derek and Geri agreed. Bobby and Francois invited even more people to hang out at the studio with them to show off their involvement with the project. Sara spent less time with Francois, devoting her attention completely on the music she was making with Derek and Geri.

One day, Irving, an investor and one of the people hanging out at the studio, took Francois aside and told him that he really liked Sara's potential. Irving explained that he made millions speculating in real estate and wanted to invest in the band. Francois, sensing an opportunity, accepted $50,000 from Irving to be used for band expenses in exchange for 20 percent of the band's earnings. Francois promised Irving that for an investment of this size, he would be named the executive producer of the album and made a silent partner in the entire business of the band, including all income earned from the band's eventual record deal, the band's studio, and all live performances. Francois signed a short letter of agreement drafted by Irving's lawyer on behalf of the group and didn't tell anyone else about the deal. Irving got tired of the monotony of the recording process, so after a week of hanging out, he went off to work on his other investment opportunities, knowing that his ownership stake in Sara's career was secure.

Several months later, the project was finished. A number of reputable record labels were interested in signing Sara as a solo artist based on the brilliant recording featuring songs co-written by Sara, Derek, and Geri. Bobby and Francois never improved as musicians, so their tracks weren't included anywhere on the recordings. Sara explained to Bobby that she let him participate in the project so he could develop his musicianship skills while they bonded as siblings. Bobby thanked her for helping him "find himself" during the process, realized that he would never be dedicated enough to be a great musician like her, and went off to enroll in culinary school to become a pastry chef. Francois, upon finding out that his tracks were not used in the final mix of the recordings, was angered. In a fit of rage, he broke up with Sara, trashed the recording studio, threatened to "get" Derek and Geri for cutting him out of the band, and, in a final effort to hurt Sara, said that he was going to have to be cashed out before allowing her to leave the band. Two weeks later, Francois married a woman he met during the recording sessions.

Shortly after the Francois incident, Sara signed a deal with one of the major labels that heard Sara's demo. DG Music Productions was asked to stay on and produce the entire album for Sara. In fact, the label was so impressed with the writing, production, and professionalism of the team of Sara, Derek, and Geri that they offered a production deal to DG Music Productions and advanced Derek and Geri half a million dollars to find and develop six acts over two years for the label. Derek and Geri were so grateful to Sara for being the artist to showcase their talents that they offered her a partnership in their business. Sara declined, knowing that she would be very busy on her own career, content that she had something to do with DG Music Productions finally getting the professional recognition it deserved.

When first single was being circulated to the public and press began to generate for Sara's record release, Francois and Irving emerged to discuss how they were going to get paid as partners in the deal. Both insist that they will do whatever they have to do to stop Sara's release from coming out until they are "taken care of." What are Sara, Derek, Geri, and the record label going to do now?

Going It Alone

The Lone Wolf, the Little Red Hen, One Little Indian, the Solo Act... call it what you like, the most basic business entity is the *sole proprietorship*. As the name describes, this is an entity of one person doing business by himself or herself. The reasons for doing business as a sole proprietor are many. It could be because you want to have complete control of your own destiny. Or, like the Little Red Hen, maybe you think that if you do all of the work, you should be the only one who deserves to reap all of the reward. Many times, musicians choose a sole proprietorship as a business entity simply because no one else shares their artistic or business vision, and they're forced to carry out all of the duties of their business by themselves.

When I ask people why they chose to take the sole proprietor route, the most frequent answer is that they love the independence, the feeling that they don't have anyone to answer to but themselves. This is great if you are truly self-motivated, can set and keep goals on your own, and can evaluate your own progress. You get to retain all of the control of your business and you get to keep all of the profits. Sounds pretty good so far, doesn't it?

However, there's a down side to being out on the business limb all by yourself. Just as you receive all the reward, you also assume all of the risk. Furthermore, if your business grows, you may not be able to manage it all by yourself. Your creativity and output may suffer if you also have to do the promotion, return all the calls, and balance the books as well as practice, create, and produce. It is *possible* to handle all of the work related to your career by yourself, but make sure you consider whether or not you actually *like* doing the various necessary jobs and whether you have the skill set to do all of them. Not only does division of labor help when growing a business, but being able to bounce ideas off of another person does, as well. If you should decide to do it alone, be sure that you have access to other businesspeople with which you can share your ideas and troubles. Setting up your studio or office in a location where you can run into others running small businesses helps. So does joining professional groups or associations to network and swap notes. A support group of like-minded people can go a long way toward battling the isolation that sometimes accompanies being a sole proprietor.

Procedurally, establishing yourself as a sole proprietorship requires very little paperwork. If you choose to do business under a fictitious business name (such as a band or production company name that is not your legal name), you will have to file a fictitious business statement in your municipality. Doing business in the music industry is almost sure to take you beyond the borders of your home town, so be sure to review the section in Chapter 2 about the need to establish and protect your trademark if you are using a fictitious business name (a business name used by sole proprietors instead of their personal name). Opening a bank account, establishing credit, and signing contracts as a sole proprietor are all easy to do because you don't have to wait for others to approve or sign agreements or forms with you.

When you do business or enter into agreements with other people or companies as a sole proprietor, make sure that your agreements include language stating that you are not partners or any other business entity that may obligate you to them beyond that one project. A certain amount of "professional distance" needs to be kept from the people you work with, regardless of how close you may be as friends and fellow artists, in order to maintain sole proprietor status.

A common example of what I refer to as an inadvertent partnership occurs when a solo artist works with a backup band of musicians. It gets especially sticky when the backup band members are paid little or no money during the "dues paying" growth period, and then the act is presented with an artist deal or some other kind of professional opportunity. In the eyes of the solo artist, she is a sole proprietor who was hiring the services of independently contracted musicians with no ties to her career. The band members, however, may be characterizing the relationship as a partnership with the solo artist, requiring a "buy out" in order to let the artist move forward with her career without them. Although it may seem like a time-consuming and expensive formality in the beginning stages of a solo artist's career, the best bet is to establish from the outset that the musicians are independent contractors who are providing their services to you on a work-for-hire basis and get paid by the job. The use of musician releases (discussed in Chapter 10) is helpful in making sure that you own the fruits of the labor that these independent contractors have provided, and that you have the rights to use the performances, names, and likenesses of your musicians on recordings that you make with them. It will be much cheaper and less time consuming to take care of these details as a sole proprietor than attempt to undo an inadvertent and unwilling partnership in the future.

Partnerships: All for One, One for All

The next business entity to consider is the *general partnership*. While the formalities of establishing a general partnership vary from state to state, in very basic terms, any time you have two or more people acting together toward a common business goal, they are considered a partnership.

A partnership has many potential benefits over a sole proprietorship. On the creative side, collaboration can create solutions to problems and lead to dynamic growth. On the financial side, sharing information and resources with the right people can be extremely valuable, and splitting costs lowers your out-of-pocket investment. Most of all, delegating the work is the easiest way to streamline the implementation of a business plan.

On the down side, the addition of other opinions requires establishing procedures for running your business and dealing with personalities. In addition, partners are responsible for each others' actions—including potential misdeeds. This is a very important consideration, for if you are a member of a band that is doing business as a partnership and someone in the band should trash a hotel room, hurt an audience member, or infringe on another artist's copyright within the scope of the common efforts of your band, the entire band may be held liable, and therefore required to compensate the party that is making the claim, even if it's technically against only one person in the band. Absent limitations of authority in a formal partnership agreement, partners may also make contracts or take on financial responsibilities on behalf of the partnership. If your singer decides it's time to buy a new band van and does so on behalf of the band, you might be saddled with the obligation of paying off the loan for the van whether or not you thought it was a necessary purchase. If the person or dealership that sold you the van had the impression that your partnership was to be responsible for paying for the goods, that person's opinion or impression is often the one that counts.

Another potential disadvantage of a partnership is that third parties can seek each partner's personal assets to pay off partnership liabilities. If the partnership is responsible for payments to a third party, each individual partner needs to pay up, whether the money comes from the partnership business or not. Let's take a look at our "band van" example. If the lead singer who bought the van leaves the band, the partnership is still financially responsible for paying the loan on the van. Now you have a band debt and the band is not making any income while it's looking for and breaking in a new singer. If you are working as a police officer while playing in a band, the finance company that loaned the partnership the money to purchase the van can go after your personal earnings as a police officer if the band's earnings or assets are not enough to make the payments.

Corporations and Limited Liability Companies

To avoid the issue of personal liability that individuals face in sole proprietorships and partnerships, two other types of business entities are worth considering, each of which serves to limit individual liability. These business entities are *corporations* and *limited liability companies* (LLCs).

While somewhat different from each other, corporations and limited liability companies share the common purpose of limiting each individual owner's liability to only what the company owns. Looking once again at our lead singer/van scenario above, if the band entity is unable to pay off the loan for the van, the finance company would be limited to seek only the assets of the band entity rather than the individual, personal assets of each of the members of the band, as in the case of a partnership. The individual owners of a corporation are called *shareholders;* their counterparts in a limited liability company are called *members.* The primary difference between corporations and limited liability companies is that corporations are usually required to follow more formalities than a limited liability company. Some of these formalities include activities such as holding regular meetings, keeping minutes of those meetings, and filing certain documents with the Secretary of State of the state in which the corporation is established. Some states are much more corporate-friendly than others—particularly when it comes to taxation—so businesses are often formed in one state but have its owners and primary business based in a different state.

Joint Ventures

One final business entity worth mentioning is called a *joint venture,* often referred to as a *JV.* Essentially, the joint venture is a partnership with a very limited scope or purpose. For example, if a production company were to record a master, and a marketing company were to market the CDs, the companies could create a joint venture for the sole purpose of generating sales and sharing the profits for only that one project.

I think the joint venture is underutilized as a viable option when musicians or different types of entertainment companies work together. It allows the parties the flexibility to see how they can work with each other while not locking them into a long-term relationship right away. Each of the venturers take on separate obligations and potential liabilities for their respective components of the business, but their joint efforts can be shared based on their agreement with each other. Using our "band with the van" example, let's assume that the lead singer who originally purchased the van did so individually, taking on the obligation to pay for it by himself. If he brought the van to the band as an asset that the joint venture could use and benefit from, depending on the agreement between the parties, the remaining venturers may have to take on the obligation of paying for the van—even after he should leave—if the band venture were to continue without him. Think of it as a "living together before getting married" approach to business. If the parties should decide down the road that their JV was rewarding enough to want to continue the relationship with more commitment, they might consider forming some other longer-term entity or simply form another JV with a broadened scope (for example, three master recordings instead of just one).

Non-profit Corporations

An often overlooked but effective business entity is the *non-profit* (or *not-for-profit*) corporation. In the United States, many non-profit corporations carry the tradition of spreading the gift of visual and performing arts to the masses. Your town's opera, symphony orchestra, and museums are all likely to be non-profit corporations.

Under the non-profit corporation business model, a business entity is formed under specific guidelines and civic purposes, such as the development and sharing of art with the public through schools, public performances, or other civic programs. As an incentive for doing your civic duty, depending on the specific laws of your city and state, your non-profit corporation may be exempt from paying federal, state, or local taxes. Additionally, funding not available to for-profit entities is made available to non-profit corporations, such as grants, loans, prizes, donations, and proceeds from fund-raising activities. To take advantage of the breaks given to non-profit corporations, you need to research your state's laws and guidelines for the formation of non-profit corporations and follow them to the letter; otherwise, you will lose your tax-exempt status.

If you choose this form of business entity, it is very important to remember that the terms "non-profit" or "not-for-profit" do not necessarily mean that you are required to lose money. On the contrary, non-profit organizations that perennially work in the red often lose their non-profit status because they are not run like a solid business enterprise. Remember that the term "non-profit" only refers to the type of business entity you have, not whether you earn any money. Many extremely successful enterprises are non-profit corporations.

Deconstruction

Let's face it: All good things eventually come to an end, including even the best bands or other musical ventures. While this is a somewhat fatalistic attitude, I think it's a realistic one and should be considered at the inception of a business entity. There should be no hidden surprises to anyone when a member leaves or if the band should break up.

With this in mind, it is a good idea for everyone involved in the entity to get together and rationally talk over the hard issues associated with breaking up the act. A colleague of mine who specializes in mediations holds a special mediation session with bands relatively early in their relationship to discuss these deconstruction issues, well before anyone is even thinking about taking the band apart. This way, clear minds prevail and band members can explore a number of "what if?" scenarios in a civil, non-emotional environment. If an issue never comes up in their future, then they never have to resort to looking at the document; if some problems arise, then they have a road map to refer to when trying to resolve the issues.

Get It in Writing

So what kind of document is necessary to establish your business entity once you have chosen it? You need a document that spells out the inner workings of the business entity, from how the ownership is split to how to remove members from the group. The type of document you draw up depends on which entity you set up. Partnerships have *partnership agreements,* LLCs have *member agreements,* and corporations have *by-laws.* All three documents serve the same purpose: to create a procedural foundation on which to build the success of a musical business.

Regardless of the business entity that you choose to form, the emphasis here is on the word "written." Citing a variety of reasons, ranging from the inability to commit to possessing a casual artist attitude, musicians often avoid putting their business entity agreements in writing. Not having such a document can be both sad and costly if the business arrangement needs to be sorted out. There is nothing like witnessing the implosion of a creative partnership that earned millions of dollars whose only documentation of their partnership was a handwritten agreement given to the bank to open an account when they cashed their first group check years before their demise.

Besides the requirements to file the formal documentation necessary for certain business entities, the benefits of a written agreement between those in business together are enormous. Being able to simply look at a document to clarify any issues does wonders for relationships. In addition, I find that sometimes creative types need to regularly revisit their goals, procedures, and "success road map" with each other. Referring to a mutual agreement to succeed together is one of the best ways to replenish the energy and focus needed in the music industry. First of all, the timing of drafting and executing a formal document is a touchy subject. Think of it as being similar to discussing marriage with someone you like. When is the right time to bring up the legal issues, formal business issues, and hard questions about breaking up—especially when you are having so much fun? My personal and professional opinion is that the issues should at least be discussed early on in the relationship so no one is strung along thinking that a future opportunity exists when in reality, one doesn't exist. It's only fair, and it breeds the kind of communication that results in successful business and artistic entities.

When you mutually arrive at the right opportunity to discuss your formal future together, there are a number of important issues to think about and include in your document, regardless of the form of business entity that you choose. Remember that the aims and dynamic of every business entity are different, so take some time to think carefully through what works for each of you individually as well as what works for your group as a whole. Here are a few of the issues that your document should address:

- *Who are the core members of the business entity*? Are there "senior" members and "junior" members based on time invested in the collective, certain skills, or financial investment in the entity? Are people who were involved with the business prior to the formal formation of the business going to be left out of the entity? Do they need to be compensated or "bought out" in any way?

- *Who owns the trademarks of the entity?* Does the entity own the trademarks that identify it? If a person leaves the entity, can they use the trademark? If the act stops doing business with each other, can any of the co-owners use the trademark? Is the trademark held in trust, leaving none of the parties the right to use the name but all being able to participate in earnings from property that is created using the trademarks of the entity?

- *How is property owned and held by the business entity*? Who owns copyrights co-written by partners in the company? Are they owned and administered by the entity or by each individual contributing member? When purchasing major items like equipment or paying for studio time, does the entity make these payments or reimburse the individual who purchased the items or services? How is co-owned property maintained and disposed of when no longer of use to the entity?

- *How much does each individual own of the company?* While it's easy to smile at each other and chant how everyone is even, sometimes the reality is that an uneven contribution of cash or sweat equity may result in an uneven distribution of ownership rights. Is there a formula that can be implemented to reward uneven contributions and/or ownership in the entity?

- *How does the entity make decisions?* Does seniority or a higher stake of ownership affect making company decisions? Are there different levels of decision making? For example, choosing what color paper to tell the copy shop to use for your promotional flyers might not be as important as choosing what record label to sign with. Do both decisions require one person making the decision for everyone else? A majority? A unanimous decision? Can a decision be overruled? How?

- *Is there a minimum financial contribution to be made by each individual to join the entity?* Do the original members have to exchange money, property, exclusive services, or something else of value to be a part of this business? How is this valued? Do future co-owners have to make similar contributions? Can the entity use this contribution to run the business or not?

- *How are partners added or subtracted?* This is by far the most difficult discussion that creative individuals can get into when contemplating the formation of a business entity. Is a person who voluntarily leaves treated differently from one who is asked to leave? Are there buyouts? How do you determine how much the buyout is going to be? What happens if a partner dies? If a partner is married, does the surviving spouse become a voting or non-voting partner in the entity? If the entity adopts the concept of expulsion (the legal term used for "kicking a partner out"), what grounds and guidelines are used to determine whether this can be done? Does the member have to have committed a felony before being asked to leave? To have shown up late for too many rehearsals? To have embarrassed the rest of the members? These terms are wide open, many times subjective, and negotiated heavily based on the individual and collective dynamic of all of the participants in the business.

- *What is the purpose of the business?* Is your business entity an umbrella for a variety of entertainment-related businesses or is it formed for a very specific purpose? For example, in the case of a band, business entities potentially can include the collective formation of a performing group, a publishing company, an independent production company and/or label, a merchandise company, or a business that has nothing to do with the music industry. Specifically identifying the purpose of the entity not only limits the scope of what businesses the individuals will participate in, but also sets limits on what the business will be liable for when individuals act beyond the scope of the business. For example, if the specific scope of the business is to write and publish musical compositions, the company may be responsible if a partner infringes on a third party's copyright, but it is likely not to be responsible for the damage done by the same partner if she gets into a bar fight with a third party because someone didn't like her song. Writing songs is within the scope of the business; getting drunk and fighting is not.

- *How long should the business last?* Is it being formed for a set period of time, is it perpetual, or is it limited in the time it takes to deliver a certain amount of entertainment product? Are there specific goals that must be met for the entity to continue? Do the individual participants have to decide periodically whether the business keeps going or not? If certain participants leave (for example, if the primary members of a band split off to form another band), will the entity dissolve or continue?

- *Is there an agreement not to compete?* Are the skills and activities of the individual members of a business entity so unique and valuable that they should be restricted from providing those services to third parties outside of the business? For example, if a production team intends to build up its reputation as a team, would the entity benefit from restricting the individuals from competing with each other? If there is an agreement not to compete, it needs to be clear, fair, and not be so restrictive that a person cannot make a living because of the restrictions.

- *What warranties do the individuals have to make and what indemnification procedures are to be implemented?* When entering into business relationships, individuals make promises to each other that are relied upon in order for the entity to function without the cloud of third party liability lurking over it. Individuals usually make certain warranties to each other regarding important considerations, such as the ownership of property brought into the business venture; that no other agreements or relationships exist that restrict them, so they are free to enter into the business; and that they will not subject the business to third party liability due to their actions. If these warranties and promises are not kept and the business turns out to be liable to a third party because of the flawed warranty, the individual making the warranty usually *indemnifies*—or pays back—the business for any losses or liabilities to third parties that are a result of the warranty. Going back to our "band with the van" example, if the singer warranted to the band that he owned the van outright when he still owed money to a finance company, and the band ended up having to pay for the balance plus any additional costs that the finance company required, the band could seek indemnification from the singer because his warranty was not a valid one.

- *Does the entity have insurance?* Does the entity secure against any potential loss or liability by taking out insurance policies for the health/life of individual members, for property that is co-owned, or for liability purposes? For example, what if a member of a group dies suddenly and the group cannot continue? Does the group simply go out of business or can the remaining members utilize the proceeds paid to them as beneficiaries of a "key partner" life insurance policy to hire the proper personnel to keep the business going or move on in their individual endeavors? If a member of a group were to be found liable for assaulting a disruptive audience member, would the liability insurance coverage of the group protect the other members from having to pay the third party?

- *What is the dissolution procedure?* What steps are to be taken when the business is extinguished? A common problem is that if a creative entity like a band has experienced any kind of success at all, various products have been produced that will continue generate income well after the bandmates stop talking to each other. If no steps are taken after the band breaks up (for instance, appointing a trustee or business manager to collect and distribute income to the individual band members), future earnings may remain in a state of dispute.

While the major issues I've outlined here are not exhaustive, they should serve as an introduction to the types of issues involved in putting together an agreement to form and run your business entity. The key to an effective document is for all participants in the business to anticipate as many potential scenarios as possible for the success and failure of the business. Sharing personal and professional plans at the outset of a business relationship makes for a better and smoother ride as the opportunities and challenges unfold.

Companion Questions

1. *Do you like working alone or is working with other people important to you?*

2. *Who owns the name of your band or business? Who gets to continue to use it when a member leaves or the entire entity is dissolved?*

3. *Are partners making an initial cash contribution and/or a continuing contribution to the entity?*

4. *What kind of personal assets does each person own? Do they want to protect those individual assets from third parties?*

5. *Are members making contributions other than cash to the partnership, such as equipment, rehearsal space, or recording studio access?*

6. *If some members are making non-cash contributions, is there a procedure in place to have other members "match" the contribution with either cash or similar non-cash contributions?*

7. *Is there a procedure for repayment of non-cash contributions?*

8. *How are members added?*

9. *How are members removed?*

10. *Is there a procedure in place to value the entity and "buy out" a member who leaves?*

11. *Is there a difference between leaving voluntarily and leaving involuntarily?*

8 | Other People's Money

Have you found yourself in that uncomfortable situation where the only obstacle between your musical dream and its completion is money? A half-mixed recording, a truck with a broken axle, a fried P.A. system, or an unpaid producer are not glamorous benchmarks of superstardom, but in the real world, these and other similar occurrences happen. Many a tour, demo project, studio, independent record release, or music-related business has fallen by the wayside because of lack of funds. If this is your dilemma, maybe it's time to think about going beyond your immediate resources and obtaining third-party money to bring your project to fruition.

The music business is just like any other business—it takes money to run it. From nominal scholarships donated by family members for piano lessons to the multimillion-dollar corporate underwriting of a national tour, there are a wide variety of money sources available to musicians. Unfortunately, much has been made in the media of entertainment money deals that have gone sour, making both investors and those seeking investors distrustful of each other. If you are well informed and prepared, working with someone to finance your project doesn't have to be an antagonistic situation. Before making important money decisions with other people's money, you should consider a number of business and legal points.

Hypothetical Situation: Attention Deficit Spending
Attention Deficit Spending (known to their fans as ADS) is a four-piece rock band that formed when the members were all college students. By the time ADS was two years into its existence, the band was a popular local act, playing cover music at college parties while

working on a demo tape of its own songs. Unfortunately, by this time the band members collectively managed to run up considerable credit card debt making purchases for their band and were having difficulty keeping up with their bills.

A friend of the band, Larry Loner, heard about the plight of ADS and offered to help out. Larry offered to loan ADS $20,000 to pay off the band members' credit cards and help finance their demo. Saying he was their biggest fan, Larry told them that he didn't want any more money than the credit card companies were getting and asked only that they pay him back when they "got their first gold record." He was confident that in time ADS would be rich, famous, and well able to pay off the loan. In exchange for his generosity, ADS wrote Larry a letter of thanks, promising to give him a gold record with his name on it one day, pay him the same interest rate that the band members were paying on their credit cards (19 percent annually), and grant him 20 percent ownership of the songs on the demo that he financed.

ADS spent the next six months finishing its demo and then set out for a year of touring around the country as an opening act for bigger bands. ADS thought it would be a good idea to sell a self-produced CD along with their T-shirts and other merchandise to make extra money while touring. Coincidentally, a week after making this decision, ADS met Chuck Bucks, a retired record label executive. Chuck told ADS that he'd invest enough money to record five masters and manufacture 5,000 CDs in exchange for 25 percent of the gross of all sales of the CDs and an equal piece of any deal that included the CD in the future. With these five masters added to its existing demo, ADS had enough tracks to sell the project at their gigs as a full-length CD. ADS jumped at this opportunity, signed a short CD investor agreement with Chuck, finished the full-length CD between tour dates, and sold these CDs on the road for the next year.

An avid fan, Mony Deluxe, contacted ADS and told them she had a rich aunt who made a lot of money in real estate and wanted to "buy her way into" the music business. Mony arranged a meeting with the band, the aunt, and the aunt's lawyer. Aunt Banque offered ADS $200,000 to become the "executive producer" of the band for three years if it would give her a 30 percent ownership stake in the band, make her the managing partner of their partnership, and put Mony on the payroll as her personal assistant for $25,000 during the first year of the investment. ADS signed the executive producer contract and let Aunt Banque know how much the band members appreciated the input from someone who was so successful in business. Aunt Banque and Mony immediately bought ADS some new instruments, recording equipment to produce a new CD, and a van for touring. They then set out to expose ADS to the public by hiring a public relations firm and a record promotions company. Aunt Banque and Mony further promoted the band by allowing a major motion picture studio to use one of the band's demo recordings on a movie for free in exchange for the band's appearance in the film. The soundtrack for the movie sold more than 850,000 units.

Within a year of partnering with Aunt Banque, ADS had a number of the major labels bidding to sign the band to an artist deal based on the band's exposure in the movie, the new ADS project recorded in the studio financed by Banque, and the buzz about the band. The band's first independent CD sold 15,000 units through independent distribution channels. ADS decided on signing with one of the major labels that wanted to re-release the first album as well as make a substantial investment into the completion and promotion of the band's second album. It was now dealing time.

Mony and Aunt Banque decided that it was a great time to cash in on their investment, so they asked for a separate one million dollar advance to be paid to them to give up their executive producer status. The label agreed, adding the advance for Aunt Banque and Mony to the money that would be recoupable from the ADS future royalties. Chuck Bucks came knocking for his 50 percent of the new deal, as well. Seeing all of the media reports about the pending ADS artist deal and the success of the movie angered Larry Loner. He lamented that he gave the band its start and that the band members forgot about him when they got their gold record for the movie. He demanded that his loan (which by this time more than doubled) be paid back immediately and that he get his piece of the songs on the original demo. Larry also threatened a copyright infringement suit against the movie producers and the record company that put out the soundtrack recording unless he was paid "a lot of money" because he didn't give them permission to use "his" 20 percent of the song in the movie.

The label is now reconsidering signing ADS because of the threatened lawsuits and the possible mounting costs that it would take to sign the band. ADS simply wanted to make ends meet as the band was making its ascent in the industry, and the band's reckless use of other people's money is now coming back to haunt it.

The Five Financial Fallacies

Let's first look at some of some of the misconceptions about the financial side of making music. In the couple of decades I've worked in the industry, I've heard a few phrases about money and music often enough that I am compelled to discuss them before going any further. I call these phrases "The Five Financial Fallacies." These are negative thoughts about money that can become self-fulfilling prophesies for musicians trying to carve out a career in the industry. I can't tell you what to think, and I can't change your belief system. Invariably, the musicians who believe these fallacies have a hard time with money even after they become successful, and those who don't accept them develop a healthy attitude about money and music.

- **Fallacy Number One:** *"It doesn't matter if I fail. I'm getting the money from a rich guy just looking for a write-off."* The person who thinks this way is starting out expecting failure. Remember that there's a difference between taking a calculated risk and admitting failure from the start. The investor is willing to take a risk, and it makes business sense to get the best possible tax benefit from every venture. This includes writing off an investment for the tax years that the venture is investing in itself or losing money. However, don't confuse this wise financial planning as a desire to lose money. Repeat after me: No one ever became rich trying to lose money. An investor can't keep losing money forever, because either the investor will run out of money, or after several years of the investor losing money, the IRS will treat the losing business as a hobby. Take a hard look at how you characterize yourself in the music business before bringing a businessperson into it with you.

Decide whether your music is a hobby or a business, embrace that decision, shoot straight with your investor, and proceed accordingly.

- **Fallacy Number Two:** *"Corporate executives are in it only for the money."* Musicians often feel that there is a line of demarcation between art and commerce that a person consciously crosses to turn their back on "the Good Guys" on the side of creativity. I know a lot of entertainment industry executives who got into the business with the love of music as their main incentive. After getting jobs in the industry, one of the duties usually found in their job descriptions is to protect the investment of their investors and to generate a profit. Why should a person be negatively judged for doing their job well? Having a title doesn't mean that a person totally abandoned the artistic side of the music. They simply have to factor in how the music fits into their job duties and goals. Music is a highly competitive and risky business in which under the best of conditions and intentions still produces more projects that lose money than make money. Executives need to be concerned about all of the aspects of their businesses—especially the bottom line. Before judging an executive's motivations, look at their track record and treat them as a human being first.

- **Fallacy Number Three:** *"I don't need to figure out right away how to pay back these four credit cards and the people who loaned me money for my career; when I have a multiplatinum record, I'll have millions of dollars to pay them off!"* Paying back debt at credit card interest rates or repairing a damaged credit rating can take years; repairing personal relationships due to unpaid loans can take even longer. Promising to pay back loans from your music business without having an understanding of how money is earned in the music industry is simply irresponsible. Excessive and uncontrolled debt can be a one-way ticket to a financial morass that could haunt you financially and emotionally for a long time. If your debt structure is out of hand to a point where it runs your life, you might have a debt problem. You should consider seeking professional help or a support group if it is out of control.

- **Fallacy Number Four:** *"Rich people are bad people."* People sometimes use this belief as an excuse not to succeed; they don't want to ever become a bad person and the easiest way to avoid becoming a bad person is to not make money. Fear or loathing of success is one of the main reasons people fail in the music business. It is simply an unfair stereotype. You might as well say, "All bass players show up late," "Women can't play the drums," or "All Germans steal." Some of my best friends are rich, and I feel that they are great people. Some had hit records, some earned their wealth by working for others, some inherited it, and some made money with their own businesses. However they came about obtaining their fortunes, they didn't suddenly become jerks when their incomes exceeded a certain dollar figure. The same applies to you. Simply vow not to change if and when you succeed financially. A good guideline is to commit to your own value system regardless of your net worth, embrace the eventuality of your reward, and then follow through on those things that bring the reward.

- **Fallacy Number Five:** *"I'm not worthy."* This fallacy has endless variations, such as the starving artist, the struggling musician, and the poor soul who gave it all up for self-expression. They all lead back to a very strong belief that doing what you love and being financially successful are mutually exclusive. They are not. Just because you're not generating millions of dollars from royalties doesn't mean you need to be making zero for your efforts. There are thousands of choices between being a struggling artist and being a huge superstar; the key is to find where you realistically fit into the spectrum. A career in the music industry isn't an all-or-nothing proposition; just be realistic and clear about your needs, wants, and vision of success.

Preparing for an Investor

If there is any project in your career that requires careful pre-production, I highly recommend that you rank submitting a proposal to a third party for funding high on the list. Whether you scribble a pitch for cash on a napkin in a restaurant or craft an elaborate formal presentation with full-color graphs, charts, and multimedia fireworks, the plan for how you intend to make money from your artistry needs to be clearly conveyed—first to yourself—and then to a potential investor. In order to do this, your proposal must contain some key basic elements so that you can negotiate in solid financial terms rather than unclear daydreaming terms. Because of securities laws, depending on the method you take to seek investors (particularly if you are obtaining money from people that you don't have a pre-existing relationship with), you may also have to file additional documents with or obtain permits from your state and/or include certain disclosures in your proposal required by your state or even the federal government.

The process of drafting your proposal will also be a good tool for you to objectively take a step back and evaluate what you are intending to do with your artistry and with your money. Often, musicians are so happy to simply be creating or playing music they don't give a lot of thought to where their money comes from and where it goes as long as they can somehow sustain a living. The proposal helps dramatically with the reality check of accountability to a third party. Some of the major points you may consider when drafting a proposal include:

- State with a high degree of detail how you earn, or propose to earn, your money. Examples could be selling recordings, songwriting, performing live, producing records, or owning a recording studio. If you have a track record for your earnings in any or all of these arenas, include it. If not, you may want to research how others have done so and include realistic projections of how you plan to earn your money. This demonstrates how serious you are about your goals and lets investors know that you understand your business.

- Let the investors know how you plan to use their money. Will it be to purchase equipment, pay yourself a salary, pay for studio time, buy your recordings or musical compositions back from a record label or publishing company, hire other musical professionals, or implement a marketing plan? Include concrete examples with real dollar figures in your proposal to help the investors evaluate your plan. Include estimates and competitive bids from vendors so you can demonstrate a range of costs.

- Identify the scope of the investment. Will the investors be involved with your career on a short-term, project, or long-term basis? If short term, perhaps ask the investors to be involved only in a specific project (e.g., an audio recording meant for sale to the public). If longer term, then the investment may be tied into your career earnings over a certain mutually fair period of time commensurate with the dollar amount and what activities you plan to engage in with the assistance of the investment. This is sometimes referred to as a "360 deal," which includes all of the artists' activities. (See Chapter 4 for more about this new type of agreement.) All of these variables can be clarified by specifying the scope of the investment.

- Demonstrate how you plan to pay the investors back if their involvement requires being paid back. This is discussed in more detail as we look at the various types of investments below, but at the root of your proposal is a repayment plan. Return on investment (ROI) is a significant factor for an investor to even consider backing you, and you owe it to someone supplying you with money to explain how much they could make and how long it will take them to receive their return for their investment.

- Warn the investors of the risk involved in your project. Once again, securities laws may require that you clearly state the nature and severity of the risk involved with your proposal. Optimism is one thing; stretching the truth too far for the law is another. Even the greatest musical projects featuring the best artists have a chance of failing. How many times have you seen major label artists follow up a multiplatinum recording or tour with a flop? It simply happens and you are not exempt. It's only fair to let an investor know that their money is at risk.

As you can see, a good plan is essential for your own and an investor's evaluation of the feasibility of an investment in your artistry. It is advisable to enlist the aid of an attorney familiar with corporate and securities laws if you will be raising money with your plan—especially from people you do not know personally. The opinions and documentation that you could gain from engaging an experienced professional to help you will pay dividends when it comes to staying clear of securities violations or having to sort out investor issues down the road.

Characterizing the Cash

When using third-party money for your project, it is crucial that all parties involved understand the intentions and expectations of the financial arrangement. Clearly determine whether the money you are receiving is a gift, a loan, or an investment with an eye toward ownership or some kind of a financial return. This one determination is crucial in determining whether and how much the outside money source will be paid back when your project turns a profit. What follows is a very brief discussion of the types of money sources, the legal relationship between the money source and the artist, and how the money source is dealt with by an artist.

Contrary to popular belief, the custom of patronage did not die after the Renaissance. People still support the arts with financial gifts. They might be friends, family, or total strangers who simply want to see you succeed because they believe in your art. I have a friend who is not unusually wealthy and has the same day-to-day financial responsibilities that most middle-income individuals do. One day he decided that he wanted to patronize young painters. So he did. With no expectation of return on investment, he sought out up-and-coming painters whose work he enjoyed and handed them nominal amounts of money to support themselves as they pursued their art. He is contributing to the world's culture. He is encouraging artists. Most of all, it makes him feel good.

In legal and financial terms, if you encounter such an angel as I've just described, the financial transaction is characterized as a *gift*. The money source is called a *donor*, *grantor*, or *patron*. You are the *beneficiary* or *grantee*. If this relationship is what the two of you have clearly agreed to, the person giving you the money is owed nothing except the courtesy of a thank you. To avoid any confusion later down the road, you might want to follow up your thanks with a thank-you card or follow-up letter acknowledging the gift and a confirmation that it is your understanding that no repayment is expected. You could show your gratitude with perhaps a "special thanks" or even some kind of title such as "executive producer" or "bankroller" in the liner notes of a recording, but that's the extent of your obligation as long as you are both clear that you are not obligated to return the money.

If there is an expectation of repayment—either with or without interest—the financial transaction is characterized as a *loan*. The money source is referred to as a *lender* or *creditor*. You are the *debtor* in this relationship. Whether the lender is a conventional source, such as a bank that issues you a personal loan or a credit card, or an unconventional source such as a family member or a fan, the basics of loans are the same. The lender is owed the *principal* amount (the amount that he lent to you) plus a negotiated interest rate usually based on how much you borrowed, the risk that the lender is taking, your credit history, and how long you are going to take to pay the lender back.

Loans will often require some sort of collateral or security to ensure that if the lender does not get his money back in accordance with the terms of the loan, something of value can be sold to recover all or part of the borrowed money. Collateral can be tangible items such as recording equipment or a classic guitar collection. It can also be relatively intangible, such as the copyrights to your recordings or songs, which may or may not have value at the time you borrow the money or default on the loan. I am very protective of clients' copyrights and advise clients not to use their songs or masters recordings as collateral for loans.

Formal or not, the terms of the loan should be in writing for all to see and understand. Most institutional lenders use relatively standard loan documentation. When using a non-traditional lender, I suggest drafting a promissory note that sets out the terms of the loan. Negotiable points of loans include interest rates, penalties for late payment or non-payment, what kind of collateral is being used to secure the loan, and what happens in case of a default. Another negotiable item of note is whether the lender can sell or assign your loan to third parties. A third situation to consider is whether the money is provided in exchange for a portion of the proceeds generated by the project at hand. This is characterized as an *investment relationship*. The money source is an *investor*, and you are the person responsible for overseeing the investment. These investment relationships are the ones in which I see the most misunderstandings, primarily because the artist and investor failed to clarify the boundaries of the relationship at the early stages.

Time and time again, we see situations where an investor gets involved with a financially strapped artist, buying into the artist's career for a relatively small amount of money. The artist goes on to make millions of dollars, and then there's a dispute down the road when the investor tries to collect on the deal. Apparently, there's some unwritten rule that says investors should not be allowed to reap the benefits of a good deal, with observers characterizing the shrewd business investment as "taking advantage" of an artist.

Distinguished from a loan or an investment relationship is that of an advance against earnings. This is best illustrated by a very common commission-sales relationship in which an employer will pay a salesperson money periodically (e.g., monthly) as an advance against anticipated commissions. As the salesperson earns commissions from sales, the advances are returned to the employer. Investors who are into creative ventures could choose to develop a similar relationship by advancing money to be paid back and then share future earnings of the business. As with loans or an investment, the advances can be secured by an ownership interest in equipment, intellectual property (e.g., copyrights in compositions or masters), or ownership in the business. In my experience, I've found that the investor who is willing to advance monies against future earnings in the highly speculative entertainment business is usually already in the business and knows the inner workings or is sophisticated enough to get advice as well as do the homework to make informed investments. Established record labels, publishing companies, investors, and even artists looking to diversify are willing to advance money to entrepreneurs who can prove that they can convert talent and potential into profits.

Potential pitfalls abound when it comes to negotiation of money deals. Most problems stem from the two sides being unclear or unrealistic in their expectations regarding the entertainment industry and each other. Sometimes investors who are used to putting their money in investments like real estate or traditional businesses think entertainment investments can be treated in the same manner. These investors are not prepared for the highly speculative nature of the entertainment business. Conversely, it surprises me how willing some artists are to dole out pieces of their financial pie without having any idea what that pie is worth. I often encounter artists who tell me that they "gave a point to this guy, and a point to that guy, and another point to that guy," without even knowing that a "point" usually refers to a single percentage point of a royalty earned by the artist based on sales of a recording (see Chapter 4, Recording Artist Agreements). If the total royalty that the artist is to receive is 10 points and he "gives away" 6 of them in exchange for investment capital, he is almost sure to be disappointed when the royalty checks arrive. The solution for this lack of clarity on both sides of the fence is for all parties to educate themselves fully on what the variety of the potential income sources are before making a commitment.

Investors feel they are taking an extremely high risk and therefore deserve a high return. The source of income from which you will be paying an investor—your success in the industry—is highly speculative and cannot be guaranteed. Often, the investor will request that they have some kind of management role in your career or supervise a specific project in order to protect their investment. Before allowing yet another person into your "inner circle," it would be wise to clarify the extent of your investor's desire to participate in the management of your project or career. However, that doesn't mean that your bargaining position renders you unable to negotiate. For example, you don't need to exchange a piece of your business for the investment forever. Perhaps you could limit the investor to a piece of a specific project such as the profits of a particular recording project that the investor's money financed. You might also consider putting a cap on the amount that investors can receive, limiting the return to, say, 20 times the amount of their investment or some set dollar figure. Another approach would be to limit the return on investment for a certain number of years instead of in perpetuity. Pull out a calculator and project how much you could potentially earn from various sales figures and then base your negotiations on those projections.

As you can see, the role of the financial person involved in your artistic career can be complicated. The best way to avoid any problems is for you to be prepared to discuss the details of your money transaction objectively. Even though the lure of someone else's cash may make you eager to move forward, take your time and make sure the deal is right for both you and your investor.

Companion Questions

1. *If you are receiving money from an outside source for a project, is the money a gift, loan, or investment?*

2. *How much money do you need? Did you give yourself enough of a contingency to see your project though completely?*

3. *Do you have a clear plan for how you will spend the money?*

4. *Have you demonstrated to yourself and your money source how you will repay the money?*

5. *Does your money source have a clear understanding of the risk involved?*

6. *In the case of an investment, is the money source investing in a particular project or your long-term career? If the investment is limited to a particular project, have you clearly limited the scope of their involvement with documentation?*

7. *Are you to receive the money in a lump sum or will the money come in phases? Do you have to meet any contingencies or obligations to receive the money?*

8. *Are you clear with yourself about what you are exchanging for the money?*

9. *Are you clear with your money source about what you are exchanging for the money?*

10. *Is there a priority of payment? Do your investors get paid before you are paid?*

11. *Does your investor get to participate in management, executive, or artistic decisions in exchange for the investment in your career?*

9 Dispute Resolution

Deals go sour. Bands break up. Things go wrong. It is inevitable that in business there comes a time when people will disagree, resulting in a dispute. The dispute could arise because conditions have changed and one party doesn't receive what was originally agreed upon. Perhaps two parties have a misunderstanding over the terms of an agreement. Perhaps one of the parties was a liar, cheat, and a crook. The underlying reasons behind disputes vary widely, but the result is the same: A dispute exists and the parties want something done about it.

Headlines and news stories featuring big-name artists make it appear that high stakes litigation is the only way to resolve a dispute. This is deceiving because most disputes are really taken care of privately and in a civil manner, far away from the eyes of the media and the public. Once a lawsuit is filed, however, the record is open to the public, so the media can capitalize on the details of the dispute and share the dirty little secrets of the stars. While the drama of open court makes good fodder for the curious public, it might not be the best option for you. When it comes to your disputes in the business, consider a few of your other options before subjecting yourself to being an item on the six o'clock news.

Hypothetical Situation: An Ounce of Prevention

The Schizo Renegotiations (the SRs) are a three-piece rock group. They started recording their independent CD at a recording studio called Arm and a Legg Studio owned by Armand Legg, a successful independent producer. The SRs paid for the studio time, the producer, and the engineer with credit cards. Because they were paying the premium rate at Arm and a Legg, the SRs were able to get an exclusive lock-out of the studio and Armand's production skills for a month. Unfortunately, the group members all hit the limits on their credit cards and ran out of money. At that point, they had finished recording only 4 out of their 10 songs and hadn't mixed any tracks yet.

The SRs asked Armand to provide the balance of studio time necessary to finish their project on a speculation basis (see glossary), promising to "pay it all back at full price along with 20 percent" when they scored a major label deal. Armand agreed over the telephone, adding that because they weren't paying anything, he could give them time only when the studio was not booked. Thinking they had no alternatives, the SRs agreed. At the beginning of the first month of this arrangement, Armand wrote to the SRs and let them know that he could get them in for six sessions from 10 P.M. to 6 A.M., with the understanding that he could bump them if a paying customer wanted to book that same time slot. Armand also told them that he no longer had the energy for all night recording sessions, but his "right-hand man" could take care of the sessions. Armand said that the "magic" happens during the mixing process and that he would supervise all of the mixing. Because of scheduling, the SRs were able to make use of only four of the six sessions. When the sessions did happen, the "right-hand man" was a college intern who had no production experience at all. The SRs were very disappointed.

They wrote Armand a letter saying things weren't working out and they wanted to have the recordings they already paid for back. Armand called them, saying that he needed to be "taken care of" for the free sessions, so he considered the recordings to be his property until the band paid for all of the studio time. He also said that he wanted to help out the SRs because he believed in them and promised to open up more time. The SRs agreed to give it another try, signing a letter that stated that they would be speculated at least 40 more "prime-time" hours with Armand at the console and that the studio had a lien on the recordings until all the spec studio time was paid off.

This new arrangement worked fine for two weeks, until a major label act wanted to lock out the studio for six months and offered to pay for all of the studio time up front. Armand agreed, telling the SRs that all spec deals mean that they can get bumped by a major label project, and besides, the spec deal didn't say when the 40 hours of studio time needed to be available to them .The SRs don't know what recourse they have to get from Armand, the money they have already spent—the money they would have made if they started selling CDs had their project been completed—or to get an agreement with Armand to follow through on his promises.

Assess the Damage

First of all, determine whether you actually have a dispute at all. This might sound silly, but it is a legal and practical reality. Many disputes never make it past the preliminary stages of a legal proceeding because of what is called "a failure to state a cause of action." In short, there's nothing to argue about. Are you angry because of personality conflicts? Are you hurt because you wanted to wear black on stage and the rest of the band wanted to wear blue? Ask yourself whether your disagreement can be viewed and resolved objectively, and whether it requires a specific action that needs to be determined in order for both parties to proceed with the project or their careers. Short of that, you may just need to resolve your feelings instead of a dispute.

Another maxim used in the legal field is *de minimus non curat lex,* a wonderful Latin phrase that means, "The law does not cure trifles." You need to determine whether your dispute is worth the time, effort, and expense of using a third party to determine the outcome for you. Even if you vow to take your matter all the way to the Supreme Court, have you objectively evaluated whether the end result will equal what it takes—both in financial and emotional costs—to get you there?

Remedies

When resolving disputes, it is important to identify what kind of remedy you are seeking. You may be looking for damages that are measured in monetary terms. These can be *actual damages,* which refers to the amount of money actually lost by the aggrieved party;

speculative damages, meaning the money that could have been earned; *punitive damages,* an amount meant to punish one of the parties; and *liquidated damages,* a predetermined amount of money that the parties agree will be paid if there is a breach of contract. Sometimes, the law will specify a certain dollar figure for a certain action. Such remedies are called *statutory damages.*

Occasionally money does not or cannot provide appropriate compensation for a party. For example, how can one put a dollar figure on the value of a songwriter's exclusive services, especially if the writer hasn't written any songs yet? How about the value of a lead singer leaving a band under contract to make three more recordings for a record label? In these instances, aggrieved parties seek *equitable remedies.*

One type of equitable remedy takes the form of an enforceable court order that prevents harm from taking place. This is called *injunctive relief*—one party is stopped or *enjoined* from taking the harming action. An order for injunctive relief is a pretty severe remedy, so it is not an easy one to obtain. Depending on the gravity of the action being prevented and the speed in which the order is needed, a preliminary measure could be for a party to obtain a Temporary Restraining Order (a TRO) that will last a short period of time, followed by a preliminary injunction that stays in place until such time as a permanent injunction is granted or denied. An example of this process would be if a concert promoter is gearing up to present an annual three-day extravaganza for an audience of 50,000 people on a particular piece of real estate. The neighbors of the property may try to prevent the concert and future concerts from happening out of concern for the environment, and may want to avoid all of the disruption that comes along with 50,000 concertgoers. If the initial concert date is imminent, the neighbors are likely to seek a TRO to prevent the immediate concert from taking place, while at the same time try to get the court to issue a preliminary injunction followed by a permanent injunction to prevent the promotion of any concerts in the future.

Another type of equitable relief that is often used in the entertainment industry is *specific performance.* Obtaining a court order for specific performance essentially enforces the terms and conditions of an agreement to make sure that the parties follow through with their promises. For example, if a recording artist decides that they want to leave a long-term agreement with a record company for one reason or another, the record company cannot be adequately compensated with money for the loss of such a unique talent from its roster. The company will seek a court order for specific performance, requiring the artist to fulfill the entire duration of the contract. If this court order is granted, the artist cannot enter into an exclusive artist agreement with another record label due to the original agreement. The specific performance choice of remedy would also apply if a performing artist should decide at the last moment to skip a concert date. The promoter would seek an order for specific performance so the concert will go on because money damages alone for intangibles such as the promoter's reputation and irate ticket holder's feelings would likely be difficult to calculate.

Self-Help

Before seeking outside intervention, determine whether you have exhausted all of the remedies you could do on your own. You can do certain things to document your position and strengthen your case if a dispute should ever escalate beyond resolving matters yourself. If you are seeking payment for services, have you gone through at least a few standard cycles of invoicing? If you are unclear of a term of an agreement, did you try to clarify it or did you proceed and hope that things would somehow clear up later?

One of the first steps you can take toward resolving your dispute is writing a *demand letter*. A demand letter is a non-emotional statement of your version of the facts of the dispute along with a demand for some kind of action from the other party. A well-written demand letter should include an accurate timeline of the events leading up to the dispute, what you feel is actually in dispute, what specific action you want taken, and when you want the action to be taken. Whether by conventional mail, messenger, e-mail, or an overnight service, sending your demand letter with some kind of proof of receipt will be further evidence that the other party actually read your message.

You can also include what I call a *consequence line,* an action step that you plan to take if your demand isn't met. If you write a consequence line, be sure that the consequence is a rational and legal consequence. Direct or implied physical threats against someone (for example, "If you don't do what I say, I'm going to get you," or, "Watch your back if you don't meet my demands") compromise your position later and can be viewed as an illegal threat. A statement such as, "If you do not respond as requested within 10 days, I will seek any and all legal remedies available to me," is more likely to be looked upon as a reasonable consequence for you to put in writing. Whatever you include as a consequence line, be prepared to follow through with it. Idle threats are usually met with further inaction.

Crafting a demand letter is extremely helpful in sorting out the facts and the issues at hand. Multiple issues may need to be separated from each other; the reason they are all coming to a head finally is because you let them accumulate. You may find after you have laid out the facts objectively that there is no dispute at all, just a misinterpretation of facts or feelings. With a combination of clarity and communication, the objectivity and businesslike nature of a well-crafted demand letter will often pave the way for resolving many disputes.

Mediation

A popular method of resolving a dispute in a non-adversarial manner is to *mediate* a settlement between the parties. With mediation, a neutral, objective mediator or team of mediators evaluates the issues and evidence from the various parties and works together with them to try to resolve the issues. Mediators are trained to promote compromise and to stay neutral throughout the process. For mediation to work, the parties first need to agree that the purpose of their work with the mediator is to reach an agreement rather than have a clearly defined winner or loser.

Mediation services can be found in most municipalities. Check with your local bar association or business directories under "mediation services." Some arts organizations and law organizations offer mediation services specializing in art matters. If you have such a service available to you, try to find a mediator who has a subspecialty in music. This is very helpful, because such a mediator will already have a general interest, knowledge, and expertise in your field, and therefore, a clear idea of the issues at hand. You won't need to educate your mediator, so you will pay less for the service (most mediator services bill hourly) and your mediation will be more efficient and accurate.

Arbitration

Arbitration is a middle ground for dispute resolution that is less formal than a full court proceeding. Parties first need to agree to arbitrate a dispute, so neither side is there involuntarily. They mutually choose a third-party arbitrator or a panel of arbitrators to determine how their matter should be decided. Parties may or may not use lawyers to represent them in arbitration hearings, and the court's rules of evidence are somewhat relaxed, but many of the procedures and rules can be similar to a court proceeding. As with mediation, some arbitration services have specialists who are familiar with the business and issues of musicians.

Parties may agree to *binding arbitration* or *non-binding arbitration*. In binding arbitration, the decision of the arbitrator is final. Non-binding arbitration leaves room for the parties to proceed to court if they do not agree with the result of the arbitrator. Arbitration is much more streamlined and less expensive than the court process, so disputes can come to a quicker resolution than if you were to go to court.

Small Claims Court

Many municipalities make small claims court available to parties in need of third-party dispute resolution. The rules and regulations of small claims court vary from county to county, but generally what sets small claims court apart from other courts is that lawyers do not represent the parties and there is a specific dollar figure limit to how much a party can recover. Each municipality sets this limit, so you need to do some research to determine whether small claims court is the right venue for you.

If you are reading this book, you have probably performed music in front of an audience at some point in your life. If you will be going to small claims court, use the same common sense and guidelines for your day in court that you would for one of your performances. Be prepared with written material to guide you (this is where your demand letter is helpful), dress appropriately for your "audience," and be courteous. Above all, tell your story with accuracy and conviction. The judgment of a small claims court is binding and enforceable, but can be appealed if one party feels that the judgment was inadequate or the wrong interpretation of the law.

Litigation

There is a time and a place for everything, and sometimes that includes full-blown, all-bets-are-off litigation. If all other avenues of reaching a resolution appear to be fruitless, the parties can go to court to have their issues determined by a judge or a jury. But litigation takes time, expertise, gamesmanship, and money.

If you are a party in a civil lawsuit, hiring a litigator by the hour can add up quickly. One way to hire a lawyer is on a *contingency* basis. In this case, the lawyer is paid a percentage of what is awarded to the client from the outcome of the case. For a lawyer to take on a case on a contingency, you will both have to evaluate the matter to determine the likelihood and the potential amount of an award. Note that except in extraordinarily strong cases, this evaluation is highly speculative. If you are the defendant in a lawsuit and are not likely to be awarded money from the suit, it is unlikely that you will be able to hire a lawyer to defend you on a contingency basis; you are simply forced to pay out of your pocket.

In civil litigation cases, strategies are developed, rules of procedure and evidence are strictly enforced, the exchange of information, documentation, and initial witness testimony takes place in the form of depositions (oral statements) and interrogatories (written statements) as the parties prepare for their day in court before a determiner of fact. If a case is tried before a jury, a great deal of time is spent on jury selection to make sure that the trial will be a fair and unbiased one. This is especially important if one or more of the parties are celebrities about whom the jury pool may have already formed opinions.

If either party feels that a judicial error was made in a civil trial, that party can appeal the decision. Verdicts can be large at times, resulting in decisions of millions of dollars, or they can be surprisingly small, leaving the parties with little but legal bills. Losers sometimes end up having to pay the legal bills for the other side.

Heading Off Trouble

Entertainment litigation is not for the faint of heart and is a time-consuming affair. I am not for a moment minimizing the good faith effort of those entertainment lawyers truly trying to make a point, zealously representing their clients and using the court system to better interpret entertainment law issues. Based on the nature of the economics of going to court, I am enough of a realist to know that not all of the worthy cases will make it to a judge or a jury.

To avoid disputes, the best place to start is with clear communication. Carefully choose whom you do business with, have a strong sense of ethics, use solid agreements, and deal with others fairly. Despite all precautions, disputes are likely to occur. Regardless of how you choose to resolve your disputes, you need to be clear about your goals, the issues, the facts, and how much you are willing to invest to reach your desired outcome.

Companion Questions

1.   *Is legal action truly your only course of action? Can your conflict be resolved in other ways? For example, have you tried to resolve your dispute person to person, re-invoiced your client, written a demand letter, or tried mediation?*

2.   *What is your goal in pursuing legal avenues to resolve a dispute? Are you merely avoiding a confrontation that you should be facing on your own?*

3. *Is the resolution you are seeking measurable in a tangible way, such as a certain dollar amount you are owed or securing release from an unfair contract?*

4. *Is it possible that you could actually lose money by pursuing legal action, given what you stand to gain versus what you may have to spend to get it?*

5. *Is there anything you could have done at the outset of the disputed relationship to avoid legal problems down the road, such as using carefully worded agreements, not making oral agreements, or taking a period of time to evaluate a relationship before diving into it?*

6. *Are any of the parties using litigation or the threat of litigation as a negotiation tool or a method of intimidation? Can this be avoided in any way?*

Side Deals

10 Declaration of Independents: A Self-Release Checklist

A revolution has been brewing in the entertainment industry over the past decade or so that is charging forward in full force in a variety of ways. It is the revolution of the independent media companies. If you were to look all the way back to the inception of the music industry, independent companies that produce, manufacture, and distribute music have been present throughout, but since the mid-1990s, a variety of circumstances have resulted in an unprecedented explosion of indies on the entertainment scene.

It is difficult to point out any single contributing factor in the emergence of independent record companies, but it is helpful to look at a few important underlying factors to understand how the industry has arrived at this point. The economy—both locally and globally—has changed dramatically. Major entertainment companies and media companies have been consolidating since the early 1990s. The result of the seemingly endless mergers and acquisitions of these companies is that fewer of them are servicing all of the artists who have signed long-term contracts to make records. The result is that these companies have stopped developing talent, placing more emphasis on marketing and distribution of pre-developed talent. Another reason for the independent revolution is that audio and visual recording technology—once available only to major labels with huge financial resources—has dropped in price to a point where independent artists can get their hands on the equipment to create professional-quality audio visual recordings.

In my opinion, computer technology, however, has been the single most influential catalyst to the emergence of independent entertainment companies of all kinds—including music companies. The ability to instantaneously distribute, share, broadcast, market, and create communities through the network of computers all around the world has created chaos in the established music industry, while at the same time fostering a new breed of artists who are learning how to use the technology to expand their audience. The established music industry has also made some adjustments to conform to a new business model, but the industry is changing too rapidly to allow a new business standard to take hold. Historically, this is great news for independent entertainment companies. While sound, traditional business practices must be adhered to regarding fiscal matters, the opportunities for independent artists to innovatively seek audiences are seemingly endless.

The economic swing in the music business landscape is not the only thing that makes independence a viable avenue. Of equal importance are the attitude swings that have taken place. On one hand, we have the music-buying audience. Even though a significant portion of the public is still swayed by the media, there seems to be a sentiment by discerning audiences of wanting to make their own musical choices rather than be railroaded by slick advertising and mass-marketing techniques. Above all else, a number of artists are willing to take on the responsibilities of business entrepreneurs, and their fan bases support them. This attitude has grown partly out of necessity because other companies won't develop or sell their products. It has also developed out of a growing spirit of adventure, loyalty, and self-determination. Many artists can't get major labels to even acknowledge that they are alive. Other artists have been part of the major label system in the past, but no longer can generate the sales that a major label requires to continue as part of its roster.

Whatever the combination of reasons that compel you, if you are an indie, I salute your efforts and courage to put yourself on the line by taking the independent route. I also want to warn you that your legal responsibilities do not go away simply because you are not a large multinational corporation. Because so many artists are going independent or considering doing so, I felt that it was important to address some of the concerns that are common to indie labels. This chapter presents my checklist of the top 20 legal issues that you should address before you release an independently produced project for sale. Also note that because this chapter is a checklist, it doesn't include the "Companion Questions" or hypothetical situation provided in the book's other chapters.

Before you immediately read the list and start checking things off, note that each issue is not extensively detailed. Some of these issues are discussed in detail elsewhere in the book, so you can cross-reference them and get a better understanding if necessary. Finally, I have listed the top 20 in alphabetical order, not in any ranking of importance. This is because I feel that all of these issues are important to your project and you should address them all.

1. Artist Agreements

If you are a third-party indie releasing a recording of artists, you will want to have an agreement with the artist or artists appearing on your release. If you are releasing a compilation recording—a recording consisting of multiple artists on the same release—you need to have artist agreements with each artist or independent label providing you with masters.

Self-released projects in which you are a sole proprietor may not absolutely require an artist agreement. However, in a group situation, it is a good idea to have an artist agreement that addresses common third-party "label" rights, obligations, and other issues just in case your group should split up. For example, most record labels have a right to keep selling recordings of a group, regardless of changes in personnel. Unfortunately, members of groups often leave under hostile circumstances. One of the common ways for a departing member of a group to retaliate against bandmates is to withdraw the right of the remaining members of the group to sell products that use the departing member's performances, name, likeness, and biographical material. Having an artist agreement and a band partnership agreement in place that anticipates the "what ifs" of a separation can help you avoid this scenario.

2. Artwork

All printed material to be used on your project can and should be copyrighted material. This includes photos, paintings, liner notes, logos, and graphic design work. If you intend to own the artwork on your release exclusively without having to pay additional use fees and/or royalties to the artist who created the work for you, I suggest that you have the artist sign a work-for-hire agreement granting you the right to copyright the work as the party who commissioned it. Depending on the stature of the artists you are working with, work-for-hire agreements may require a buyout fee (sometimes running into thousands of dollars) above and beyond the fees involved to create the work.

In the event that you cannot obtain the copyright for your artwork via a work-for-hire agreement, you will need to secure some kind of agreement—usually a use license—to use the artwork in connection with your project. At a minimum, your license should set out the scope of your use (for example, whether it is only for use on a CD cover or if you can use it on a website or on posters, T-shirts, and other promotional materials), how much you are paying for such uses, what kind of promotional credit the artist should get for his work, and how long you can use the artwork. It is a good practice to make sure that the person who is supplying you with artwork has the right to do so and will indemnify you for any costs that you may incur if her warranty of ownership is not good.

One final important note on artwork is that logos can potentially be both trademarks *and* copyrighted material. If you intend to use artwork as a trademark, it is extremely important to secure the ownership or license rights to the artwork. Could you imagine how expensive and cumbersome it could get if you had to secure the rights to use your band logo every time you wanted to make any kind of promotional material? In order to sidestep going through this effort repeatedly, be sure to secure your artwork rights for your potential trademarks.

3. Consignment Agreements

For independent releases, a consignment deal is a commonly used variation of a distribution agreement. Retail outlets may not be willing to sell your product until you can prove that it is worth their shelf space, time, energy, and money to do so. One way to develop your relationship with a retail store is to sell your project on consignment. In a consignment deal, you supply the store selling your recording with product and you get paid only for what the store sells. The major terms of a consignment agreement include setting the retail price of your project, how much you will be paid for each unit sold, how long the store will carry your product, and how often the store will pay you.

4. Consulting Agreements

The downsizing of major record labels has led to an upside for independent labels: A number of highly qualified people are available to hire on a freelance basis. Hiring a freelance consultant with industry experience can gain you information, access, and credibility as you launch your indie product and label. Labels are hiring consultants to perform duties such as marketing, publicity, retail relations, radio promotion, and A&R coordination.

Consulting agreements typically define how long you will employ the consultant's services, how broad the scope of the consultancy will be, what the objective performance benchmarks will be, how much and when the consultant will be paid, and what kind of expenses the consultant bill to your label for reimbursement. You should be very clear on what you as a label get to use and retain as the product of the consultant's work. For example, some consultants are unwilling to turn over their lists of contacts and telephone numbers no matter how much you may pay them because they have taken years to develop these precious relationships in the industry.

5. Copyright Filings

Be sure to register the proper copyright forms for the various types of copyrighted material associated with your project. Remember that copyright paperwork does not end with just the songs (form PA) and masters (form SR) associated with your release. Make sure that you review all original material created for your release and the promotional materials for the release. Make sure that you file separate forms for your cover art and photographs, video elements, any written text associated with your project (liner notes, promotional pieces, and so on), and website elements.

6. Courtesy Letters

It is common for independent artists to enlist the aid of other artists to make guest appearances on their recordings. This sharing of talent and personality is valuable because lesser-known indie acts sometimes can associate themselves with bigger acts that have a proven reputation.

Even if the guest artist tells you that it's okay to use their performance and name on your project, the permission is probably not something that the artist can give you. Remember that if an artist has an exclusive long-term commitment to another label, he or she is likely not allowed to record for another label—big or small—without the express written consent of the label owning the rights to the artist. If the guest artist's label allows you to make a recording and use the artist's name, the label would probably want to you to give it a courtesy credit on your artwork, liner notes, and promotional materials. After you have contacted the guest artist's label and worked out the terms and conditions of the guest performance, be sure to follow up with a letter to confirm the permission.

7. Distribution Agreements

Whether plan to have your project placed in traditional brick-and-mortar stores, make hard copies available for purchase from "virtual stores," or set up a full-length release or singles for download online, it is a must to put your distribution agreement in writing. Review Chapter 11 for the basics of these agreements.

Distributors range from small one-room enterprises to the multi-national corporations that control a large part of the music industry, so distribution agreements range widely in complexity. The basic distribution terms include what project or projects the distributor may distribute; how long the distribution agreement will last; the territory of distribution; how much the distributor pays per unit; how much the distribution fee will be; how often you are paid; whether they pay you any advance money; what kind of promotional efforts, if any, the distributor will undertake on your behalf; and whether the distributor will take on the costs of manufacturing your products for you.

While still a work in progress, digital distribution of recordings is starting to come of age somewhat. Even though great strides have been made toward stabilizing this ever-changing component of the industry, standards are still being formulated. This is both good and bad news from a legal perspective. When deals are crafted around changing technology, the parties can make very innovative and creative deals. On the other hand, for the very same reasons, if a deal is made that locks in terms and obligations for any considerable amount of time, someone else is likely to come up with a better version of the deal the very next day.

If you deal with a digital distribution company directly, be sure you understand the basics of your arrangement, remembering to use the traditional brick-and-mortar method as a model. Are you limiting the time of the distribution deal? Is it exclusive or non-exclusive? Are you limiting the products? Are you limiting the format? (For example, can the distributor sell only downloads or will you allow them to sell hard copy CDs?) Can the distributor offer free clips of your music (either complete or partial downloadable versions of your works)? In the case of a download, does your project have to be sold as a complete body of work or can it be split up into components? What is your pricing going to be? If you didn't write the songs on your work intended for digital distribution, have you provided the distributor with the necessary information to notify and pay the publisher of the music directly?

A relatively new business method born from the digital distribution industry is for companies to contract with multiple independent labels, pool them together, and negotiate favorable deals for the combined labels with digital distributors. These aggregators serve as go-betweens, putting the labels and the distributors together. As with all middleman arrangements, a contract will spell out the limits of authority, length of the agreement, fees, and other conditions associated with the aggregator.

A major way in which online distribution is different from traditional distribution is that because the Internet is available worldwide, it is difficult, if not impossible, to limit online distribution geographically. Distribution deals can be extremely complicated and tricky, so enlist the aid of a consultant or lawyer, particularly if you are working on a multiple-product, multi-territory, or multiyear deal. These are just a handful of the issues that are growing every day with respect to digital distribution. Statutory rates, compulsory license fees, and web community performance and synchronization fees are all in flux and are under continual court review; be sure to read reputable industry periodicals and websites regularly to stay up to date.

8. Manufacturing and Printing Agreements

Most media manufacturing and printing companies have set policies regarding business and technical guidelines for your indie release. Read these carefully and be sure to amend them in writing if you have very specific custom arrangements for your project.

Pay particular attention to the approval process, particularly the person responsible for changes and when that responsibility arises, delivery dates, shipping charges, and all associated costs. It's also very important to establish and verify a clear chain of ownership of the intellectual property (aka your album project) being manufactured. Manufacturers now require a written warranty from the indie, guaranteeing that they do, indeed, own or control the materials being manufactured. The manufacturing and printing stage is one of the major causes of difficulties inexperienced independent labels face when getting a product out. If manufacturing gets delayed or needs to be redone because of a technical or typographical error that you approved and then discovered after the products were manufactured, it may result in a very serious domino effect on all promotional efforts for your release. Moreover, if you are responsible for the error, you may have to pay a double fee for manufacturing two sets of your product.

9. Master Licenses for Compilations

Many indies build their business by licensing previously recorded material from various sources and compiling it on one project. Usually, a compilation will have a theme to it, such as a dance compilation, songs about cars, hits of the '80s, and so on. Much like clearing a sample, you must contact each record company owning the desired masters and negotiate individual terms regarding the use of its masters. As stated previously, if the songs have already been recorded for commercial use, the copyright holders of the compositions cannot prevent you from obtaining a mechanical because of the compulsory license provision of the copyright law.

10. Mechanical Licenses

If you are using outside material for your independent release, you need to obtain a mechanical license from the copyright holder to include the song on a mechanical device such as a CD or DVD. This is especially important if the recording you are making is the first recording of the copyrighted song.

Mechanical licenses are obtained directly from the publisher, through the publisher's designated administrator, or through a mechanical license agent. Contact the publisher of your song and inquire who needs to be contacted in order to secure a mechanical license. Note that if the song has been previously recorded and released for commercial purposes (not as a demo or for sync purposes, but as a commercial release), it is subject to a compulsory license. This means that the publisher is required to issue you a license as long as you conform to the guidelines pertaining to your request that are set forth in the copyright law. If you are having some difficulty tracking down publisher ownership for songs, the proper parties and their contact information can usually be found through (1) engaging a Clearance & Licensing service, or (2) by searching the Register of Copyright database, or (3) the song databases of the Harry Fox Agency and the various performance rights organizations.

11. Money Agreements

Prior to the release of your independent recording, be sure to have all of the documentation of your loan and investor agreements in place. Investments in independent labels or recordings will sometimes take off faster than a high-tech stock, so accurate documentation can avoid investor disputes down the road.

12. Musician/Vocalist/Model Releases

Separate from the previously mentioned artist agreements are so-called *session releases* for all the people involved with your project who are providing non-royalty services, including side musicians, vocalists, engineers, technical assistants, models, and even extras on your video shoots. To use their names, likenesses, performances, and any other material associating them with your project, you should always have them sign a release acknowledging your right to do so.

Session releases typically specify the scope of the services being rendered, the owner of the product of the work, the fees involved, the limits of your use of their services (for example, a model may allow you to use her photo for your packaging, but not allow you to post her photo on your website or sell her image to anyone else), the credits to be given, and any other conditions in the future that would require further permission or payment.

If the people helping you with your indie project are doing so for little or no payment, it is wise to have them sign a release. Even if you are strapped for cash, it is better to pay a fee rather than make promises of future payments if your project takes off. So-called friends will often develop a selective memory of your deal with them only to surface at the least convenient time when they feel that you didn't pay them enough in the beginning of your career.

13. Music Publishing

One of the ways that independent labels survive on smaller sales numbers than major labels is to participate in the publishing revenue earned by the artists on the label. This is a highly specialized and completely separate business from the sales of recordings, requiring separate documentation. Whether your label is looking for complete ownership rights of songs, partial ownership rights of songs, or participation/administration rights without ownership in songs, the proper publishing agreements are necessary to secure and clarify rights.

Another publishing issue with indie releases arises when a self-released artist who writes her own songs collaborates with other writers. If the parties intend to own and administer their respective shares of the songs, I recommended that they enter into a co-publishing agreement setting out the terms and conditions of their arrangement. Generally, the parties may each deal with the co-written songs independently as long as they keep each other informed of the publishing activity and income derived from the use of their co-written songs. You can see how this might become cumbersome if they begin to duplicate efforts or have conflicting reasons for making deals regarding the songs and the master recordings of the songs.

14. Performance Rights Organizations

If your independent release is the first time you will have songs published and you didn't grant the ownership of your songs to a third-party publisher, it is time to join a performance rights organization (PRO) as a songwriter and a music publisher, if you haven't already done so. Let your PRO know what songs it should be looking for in its surveys in order to pay the proper publishers and songwriters for potential airplay and other performance royalties. ASCAP, BMI, and SESAC all have a web presence that streamlines both the application and song-reporting processes.

15. Producer Agreements

Independently released recordings usually use the services of independent producers, those hired-gun studio magicians who do not have an exclusive affiliation with any label or production company. It is extremely important to tie up all of your legal loose ends when using independent producers.

The first item of business with an independent producer is to determine whether the producer is providing multiple services. If so, it is a good idea to sort out exactly what those services are. Many producers are writers as well, so be sure that you have an understanding about where the borders are when it comes to whether or not the producer is simply producing or participating as a writer. The same goes for when the producer provides arranging services or plays on your recording as a musician. Bear in mind that when it comes to a hit record(s), the difference between being paid a flat fee as a producer and sharing in royalties as a songwriter can be literally millions of dollars.

If the producer owns the studio where you are recording, be clear about your arrangement regarding studio rental, any spec agreements, or engineering fees. It is not out of the ordinary for producers who own studios to require separate payments for the various services that they are delivering. If you work out an arrangement with a producer for a single fee to include multiple services, be sure that you know exactly what your deal includes.

Some producers ask to be paid a session fee with no expectation of a royalty, much like a studio musician. More commonly they receive a "back-end" royalty based on the sales of the project, much the same way an artist would be paid. Negotiation points of this royalty include how much the producer is paid (this varies widely; some superstar producers can garner 5 percent or more of the retail price of a recording), whether the producer gets paid from the first record sold or has to wait for the label to recoup its investment, whether the royalty is owed on gross or net revenues, and whether the producer is paid any kind of advance against the royalty. Advances for producers are like advances for artists. Demand for the producer's services and the star power of having the producer's name associated with a recording will clearly dictate how much an advance will run. Remember that if you use multiple producers for a project, you will need to enter into producer agreements with each of them individually.

16. Promotion Agreements

While somewhat related to and many times confused with publicity and public relations, third-party promotion deals require a separate agreement. Promotion of a recording project typically consists of retail, radio, Internet/new media, and video promotions, all of which are specialties. Essentially, a promotions specialist is paid to get your music played, whereas a publicity person is paid to publicize and create awareness of your act in general. Most major labels have in-house personnel to handle these promotional duties, but independents usually have to look outside the label staff to get one or more of them done effectively.

When hiring a promoter to work your record, issues to consider include the duration of the agreement (sometimes promoters work for a set period of time, others work for a "single cycle" based on how long it takes to get a single to its peak position on a radio or video chart); how much the promoter should track and report to you on the progress of his work; the fees paid to the promoter; whether those fees are based on performance (for example, getting a radio station to add a song to its playlist, achieving a certain chart position in a trade magazine, or getting chain or other stores to purchase the project); and what extra costs the label may be responsible for above and beyond the promoter's fees (such as postage and packaging to send the project to radio stations, long-distance telephone charges, and travel expenses if the promoter attends industry events on behalf of the label).

17. Publicity Campaign Agreements

With "the buzz" being a major reason an unknown act can suddenly become known to the public and sell a lot of units, the hiring of outside publicists and public relations (PR) companies is a major consideration for an indie. The development and execution of effective marketing campaigns can run into tens of thousands of dollars, which can be a major line item for an independent label.

Agreements for publicists and PR firms define what the scope of their services will be (for example, whether they are responsible for print, television, web, or all media), how long their engagement will be, how much their fees will be, when the fees get paid, whether they get bonuses for major publications or high-level exposure, what the benchmarks of performance will be, and whether or how much your label will reimburse for the costs that they may incur.

18. Samples

Sampling is the using, taking, or borrowing of even a small (identifiable) portion of a song or recording and including it in your own recording. The issue of sampling could be the subject of an entire book, so in this checklist form, I will not even attempt to cover all of the reasons, politics, philosophy, business issues, techniques, strategies, and procedures of clearing samples. I will, however, bring the basics of sample clearance to your attention. As mentioned in Chapter 3, the copyright holders of master recordings and the copyright holders of musical compositions separately own the exclusive right to make derivative works of their copyrights. This exclusive right extends to their right to prevent others from doing so. When you use, borrow, copy, reproduce, include, or alter a master recording or a musical composition—or any portion of it—by sampling it, looping it, adding or taking away lyrics or other parts of it, or changing it in any way, you are subject to copyright infringement if you do not get the permission of the copyright holders. Between the time and money spent dealing with the lawyers representing the original copyright holder, the consequences of not taking out the time to obtain a license to use a sample (also known as "clearing" the sample) can put an independent label out of business if you're not careful. An uncleared sample is the equivalent of theft; it's the use of someone else's property without permission. Aggrieved copyright holders do not take this lightly; one remedy can be for the copyright holder to seek injunctive relief by preventing the sale of the recordings that include the sample and recalling all distributed versions of the same. Another remedy can be for the original copyright holder to claim total publisher ownership, control, and rights to collect all royalties derived from the Derivative Work if the sample is not properly licensed.

Clearing the sample starts by notifying the copyright holders of your intent to change the song and/or master and negotiating the terms and conditions of their permission to make these changes. As discussed above with respect to mechanical licenses, researching the databases of the Register of Copyright, the Harry Fox Agency, or the three main performance rights organizations will usually lead to the information you need to contact the original copyright owners. Often, these terms and conditions include a flat fee or royalty payment based on sales, label credit regarding the permission granted, and in some cases ownership rights to the "new" altered song or master.

Some labels and publishing companies are very aggressive when it comes to tracking down and preventing independent labels from releasing uncleared samples, whereas others are more lenient with the "little guy" and only pursue companies that sample and sell larger numbers of units. Be aware that the uncleared sample is like a time bomb. If you reach any level of success with a project, the likelihood of your having to pay dearly for the sample goes up.

19. Studio Agreements

Nothing will shut down an independent release faster than a recording studio hanging on to final mixes while waiting to get paid. Disputes over what was or wasn't said at the beginning of a project between an independent label and studio are legendary in the industry.

If you have an arrangement with a recording studio that is anything other than a straight payment for studio time—either on an hourly basis or a flat-fee basis—it should be in writing. Speculation (or spec) agreements are common in the industry when it comes to studio rental. The basic terms of a spec deal are pretty straightforward: The artist records at a studio for free, or a reduced rate, in exchange for a speculated, premium, or back-end payment upon the occurrence of some predetermined event, such as the artist signing a third-party deal with a label. An example of a studio spec deal can be found in the hypothetical for Chapter 9. The confusion comes when the parties aren't clear about these basic terms. While not exhaustive, some of the often disputed terms include what services are subject to spec (just studio rental or the studio and personnel, such as an engineer); how much spec time will be made available; whether the spec time will be "prime time" that the studio can rent out at full rate or whether it will be during "dead hours" when the studio would otherwise be empty; what the triggering date or event of the speculated payment will be; the amount of the speculated payment; the length of the speculation period; who owns or controls the master recordings while the full payment is in limbo; and who is responsible for hard costs, such as materials and equipment rental associated with the project.

20. Trademarks

I highly recommend securing trademarks for your independent label's name, for the act's name, and for any other trade names that are associated with your project. At the very least, research the trademarks associated with your project to see whether any other companies in the music industry already use these trademarks. While I am cognizant that the costs to register your trademark may be significant—especially to an indie—balance them against the time and money involved to pull all of your product off of the shelves and remanufacture it when you need to change the label copy due to a trademark infringement. It would also be a shame if you had to change your band name and lose the name recognition you may have spent years building.

Conclusion

As you can see, the time spent dealing with the paperwork required for an independent release can sometimes be more than the time spent rehearsing and recording the project. While sometimes tedious, handling the matters with the same detail and attention that you put into a great mix will result in a true declaration of independence from the worries of unfinished business coming back to haunt you at a later date.

11 Distribution and Promotions Agreements

For musicians, the distribution and promotion of music seem to be two of the mysteries of life that are almost as puzzling as the construction of the Egyptian Pyramids. While distribution and promotion are both very important components of the music business machine, yet sometimes elusive to grasp because of the wide variety of options available, the underlying concepts behind them are not impossible to understand. Like most service providers in the industry, music distributors and promotions companies have contracts with those whom they deal with. A basic understanding of the underlying concepts, duties, and obligations behind the contracts will help you make good decisions about your distribution and promotions options.

While the two are not always tied together contractually, I chose to discuss them in the same chapter because they are somewhat related. If you are distributing music and not promoting it, the public won't think about going to purchase it. If you promote a product and it can't be found anywhere, then the promotions campaign is for naught. It's important to think about both of them simultaneously, so I took the step of doing so as well when looking at the contractual issues involved.

A Distribution Primer

First of all, it is important to acknowledge that as of the writing of the current edition of this book, the digital distribution revolution is still in the relatively early acceleration stage with much growth ahead. I've noted throughout this book that as the entertainment industry adjusts to the technology available—particularly as it relates to distribution and promotions—standards and practices change almost daily. As you read, it's important for you to understand the basic concepts while making your own mental and practical adjustments along with the industry. Think creatively and think ahead: It is the best policy for making sure that you make informed choices in your current affairs while at the same time ensuring you do not get locked into a long-term agreement that does not benefit you.

At the primary level of its definition, whoever the distributor is, whatever the means of distribution may be, and whatever form the products may take when they are being distributed, the service being performed by the distributor entails moving the product from one place to another place where it can be sold or otherwise shared. Distributors are paid a fee to move these products. From moving CDs from your garage to retail stores throughout your hometown to moving uploaded digital files in the form of recorded music and artwork to websites all over the world, the basic distribution process is important for you to understand.

It is equally important to understand what services are not included in the basic distribution process regardless of the configuration of the recording. Unless manufacturing is specifically agreed to, it is not an automatic obligation of a distributor. Traditionally, when distributors took on this role, this was known in the industry as a "P&D" (pressing and distribution) arrangement. Distributors also do not promote recordings. This, too, is an obligation of the person or company that owns and is releasing the recordings to the public. Finally, distributors do not sell music to the public. The distributor might assist in selling it to retailers, who then sell the products to the public, but ultimately, the responsibility to get the public to part with their dollars lies with the person or company releasing the recording. Do not confuse the role of distribution with any of these roles, all of which are taken on by a record label. If that record label is you as an independent, remember that it is your responsibility to take these on; do not for a minute think that if a distributor is on board, the manufacture, marketing, promotion, or sales are automatically going to happen. In short, it's important to remind yourself that the basic role of a distributor is to move the product from one place to another.

Distributors sell to different retail outlets and have built their own relationships over time to sell to those outlets. Because of this, some distributors can only get to select retail stores; others have the reputation and relationships to get to a wide variety of retail stores, from small, independent ones to major chain store retailers. When the distributor drops off the load of products at the door of the retailer, the retailer pays a wholesale price to the distributor. The distributor takes a negotiated fee for each sale—usually calculated as a percentage of the wholesale price—and pays the balance to the label. Regardless of the configuration, this is the basic distribution arrangement. With the emergence of different types of musical products requiring different types of distribution methods and technology, however, the variations on this basic distribution theme begin.

Physical versus Digital Products

At this juncture, it is important to distinguish between the various configurations of your products because the type of configuration affects the type of distributor you are going to deal with. Products that you can touch, that require literally moving them from one place to the other, are referred to as "physical" products, requiring *physical distribution*. Vinyl recordings, CDs, DVDs, and cassette tapes are all musical products that require physical distribution. These physical products can be sold through a variety of means, including computer-based sales. Think of physical sales of music products as being the same as selling baby blankets through a website. The mode of sales is digital, but the product itself is physical. Baby blankets can only be sold as physical products; they cannot be shipped to purchasers in any other form than the physical form. Websites that sell physical products still require a distributor to provide them with the physical products to sell. When a recording is reduced to an electronic configuration and is no longer a three-dimensional product that can be touched, it is referred to as a digital configuration, capable of being transmitted electronically from place to place. In this case, the "places" are computers that store the electronic data of the music. The distribution of the music in this electronic configuration is being done digitally via the Internet, world wide web, and computers, not physically with trucks. However, the ability to effectively store, upload, and account for the movement of the digital configurations of music are still necessary, so the role of the digital distributor was created and continues to develop. Note that some retail outlets sell both digital and physical products, so as you think about selling your products, keep the configurations separate and remember that distribution arrangements have to be secured for both versions.

Physical Distribution Contract Points

As with other agreements discussed in this book, when you're considering entering into a physical distribution agreement, there are a variety of terms to understand and review that are distinct from a digital distribution agreement. The following are some of the major items to consider.

Term. The length of time that a distributor gets to distribute your musical products can vary from an extremely limited period, such as a single year, to longer, multiyear terms. Both parties benefit from multiyear arrangements, as they allow the label to settle into the security of knowing that the products it produces will be available to the public, and the distributor knows that it has a steady supply of products to sell. The parties may negotiate option periods beyond the initial term of the agreement, as well. These are usually tied into sales performance; minimum numbers of products or target sales revenue from the label may be requirements to extend the agreement.

Exclusivity. Distributors may require that affiliate labels enter into an agreement on an exclusive basis. If retail outlets looking for a product can shop around for favorable pricing or treatment from more than one distributor, it may undercut the ability or incentive for the distributor to work hard for a label. Conversely, if different distributors have special relationships due to geographical proximity, specialization, or genre-specific reasons, perhaps a combination of non-exclusive relationships could be better for a label. For example, the label that produces children's music could use one distributor to supply products to retail music stores, another for bookstores, another for mail-order and children's websites, and still another for specialized children's retail stores—all based on different, specialized relationships that have been built over time.

Territory/Specialization. As already noted, distributors can be limited to geographical boundaries. This can range from being able to service local or regional retailers to having exclusive rights to distribute physical products in certain countries to worldwide distribution rights. If a distributor has an area of expertise or relationships, an agreement can be crafted to take advantage of that specialty. When negotiating with potential distributors, see if the distributor services the types of retail outlets you seek for your music. If not, find out if they are willing to follow your creative lead and establish new relationships based on your marketing and sales goals.

Fees/Price of Products. It is important to establish your fee structure with a distributor. It can be for a fixed per-unit amount that you agree upon (example: the distributor pays you $5.00 per CD that it sells to a retailer and keeps what is left) or it can be a percentage of sales (example: 30 percent of the wholesale price). Distributors will usually require that a dollar reserve be held for products that are returned to them. Another negotiating point that is very relevant with physical sales is the costs associated with returns. Shipping, warehouse fees, insurance, breakage, and other costs all add up, so policies should be established and agreed to at the outset to avoid any problems down the road.

Accounting. Anytime money is exchanged, the accounting details should be established. As discussed in previous chapters, the same principles apply with a distributor. How often is the label accounted to? Will it be quarterly, monthly, semiannually? How long can a reserve for returns be withheld by a distributor before it must be paid? Are there advances or costs that the distributor paid to the label or third parties that must be recouped? Auditing rights and minimum accounting details are important as well.

Artist/Independent Label Sales. One of the most effective retail outlets for recordings—particularly independently released recordings—are the artists or labels themselves. Artists who perform regularly or independent labels that maintain contact with their audiences through websites, fan clubs, or other creative means can sell a lot of physical product. This is a double-edged sword that is a point of negotiation with a distributor. Some distributors have no problem with artists selling their own product; others see it as undercutting the relationships that they have with traditional retail establishments in the geographical areas where the artist may be playing. A hybrid would be for the distributor to treat the artist or label as a retail outlet, provide the units to the artist or label as if it is a regular retailer at a negotiated reduced rate, and report the artist sales as if a store is selling them. Whether a retail store sells your physical product or you sell your physical product at gigs, it is a good idea to have a Universal Product Code (UPC), which is a specialized bar code printed on your units for sale. The UPC is scanned by retailers and used to track sales. This is advantageous to an artist or label that depends on reported sales for trade magazine chart positions or for the distributor to keep other retailers interested in the artist's or label's music by showing steady sales of product.

Other Points. While the major points of a distribution arrangement have now been covered, a few other details should be noted that could be made part of your agreement. It is advisable to establish the responsibility and deadlines for the creation and production of sales and promotions materials with a distributor. Establishing the "look and feel" of a record label is an important facet that should be consistent throughout the distribution and retail chain, so don't leave that to chance. Because of their relationship with retailers, distributors can introduce independent artists and labels to sales programs with retail stores that have costs associated with them. These include things like advertising, favorable product placement, sale pricing, and special marketing programs. It is important for independent artists and labels to establish how to participate in these programs and who is going to pay for them. Showcasing opportunities for artists through distributors at specific retailers, trade shows, or conferences can be explored. If the distributor is associated with a record label that manufactures physical products, the possibility of a P&D arrangement may be in order. Taken one step further, if the distributor is affiliated with a record label, don't leave out the possibility of signing an exclusive artist agreement directly with the affiliated label or selling all or a portion of the interest in your record label to the label. With the shift of major labels toward an emphasis on distribution rather than artist development, the route of a "test drive" through a distribution arrangement could be the safest route to a major label deal.

Digital Distribution Contract Points

While the smoke has somewhat cleared from the initial explosion that set off the digital distribution revolution, traditions and standards for doing business in this exciting field are far from being set in stone. Nevertheless, many digital distribution companies (also known as digital music providers or digital aggregators) have charged ahead, making great strides as they attempt to bring music to the masses via computers, digital music players, personal digital assistants (PDAs), cell phones, and other cool electronic devices.

Music can be found through a variety of avenues when e-shopping. You should be familiar with the various types of retailers so you can discuss strategies with your distributor. The first general type of music retailer is a *digital retail site* where buyers can purchase downloadable tracks of music through a dedicated website. Another type of site is an online retail store that sells music in both physical and digital configurations. These sites are known as *web retailers*. Both of these are distinguishable from *e-stores,* which are "add-ons" that allow for purchase of goods through websites that aren't primarily retail sites. An effective digital distributor needs to be familiar with all of these types of retailers in order to get your music to them and ensure the highest exposure and opportunity to sell through to the public as possible.

The inventory is still the same—music—but the configuration is no longer physical, so the means of distribution have adapted to the new form. Rather than having a warehouse full of physical configurations of products such as CDs, vinyl recordings, or tapes ready to be shipped off on trucks, the digital distributors have computers full of recordings stored in digital form ready to be shipped off electronically over cyberspace to purchasers. Digital distributors still serve the same role for labels and artists as the physical distributors, so contracts are a necessity. There are variations to the physical distribution theme that you should be aware of. Since the technology and negotiated contracts are ever changing, these contract points are likely to change as well. Some definitions relating to digital recordings can be found in the glossary in the back of this book that you may find helpful.

Term. Like the physical distribution agreements, digital distribution agreements are usually in effect for set periods of time. Since the standards for digital distribution are still a moving target, representatives on both sides of these agreements are hesitant to enter into long-term deals for fear that they might get locked into an arrangement that is not so favorable.

Rights granted to the distributor. As with physical distribution, a major question is whether or not the digital distributor's rights to sell the digital recordings are exclusive or non-exclusive. Is there a minimum amount of money that the digital distributor is required to obtain per sale or do they get to determine the price for digital distributions? Can the distributor sell to a third party who then will sell the download to the public? All of these questions become part of the framework.

Division of revenue. Some digital distribution companies will pay a negotiated wholesale price to the label (e.g., $.60 per $.99 download), while others may split the income (e.g., 60 percent of all gross receipts). In cases of subscriptions (where users of a website pay a set fee for a limited number of downloads per month, for example), a negotiated portion of the collected fees goes to the label. Ringtones for cellular phones take into account the added party of the cellular phone carrier, splitting up the money three ways on a negotiated basis among the label, the distributor, and the cellular phone company. Deciding who is responsible for payments for costs such as mechanical license fees or producer fees is also part of the distribution of income discussions.

Aggregation. Since there are so many independent labels and artists all looking for their piece of real estate on the Internet, a new digital distributor known as an aggregator emerged into the picture. Aggregators enter into exclusive term agreements with labels, prepare the music for digital distribution by digital music providers and then negotiate more favorable deals with the digital music providers because of the strength of the combined labels and artists. For this service, the aggregators usually negotiate a percentage-based fee to the labels for all revenue earned. Aggregators usually turn accountings around relatively quickly; usually on a monthly or bimonthly basis, which is much quicker than the semiannual or annual accounting method used by record labels to provide information to artists.

Promotion. Another item of negotiation with digital music providers is promotion in the way of featuring an artist on a site with interviews, by putting their video prominently on display, or highlighting an artist or label, all of which add up to the digital version of product placement of CDs in a retail store.

Whole volumes can (and have been) devoted to the ever-changing variations of digital distribution arrangements. This brief overview will hopefully give you enough of an introduction to the new model of distribution that you will carefully review and consider the importance of having the right digital distributors presenting your music to the public.

Promotions Agreements

As good as any music project can sound, if it is not promoted effectively, it will not get heard unless it is somehow promoted. Promotions can take place in a variety of different ways that independent artists and labels can utilize to bring attention to a project and hopefully increase the chances for sales. The traditional forms of promotion include radio, TV, retail, press, street, and the web.

Regardless of the type of promotion, certain key issues are usually included in agreements with the parties that provide promotional services to musicians. While not exhaustive, this brief snapshot of negotiation points may be helpful when you assemble your promotions team for a project.

Scope of performance. By far, this is the most important term of a service contract for promotional services. From specifying to a street team how many posters they are supposed to distribute for your club gig, to having a publicist deliver a written plan for how they will get you on the cover of a major rock and roll magazine, to requesting that a certain number of "friends" are added to your social networking site, a detailed scope of performance is the foundation for all parties to build a working relationship and a sound promotions plan. Minimum numbers and duration of meeting times, conference calls, and consultations may be in order. Reports or written memoranda can be discussed, as well.

Term of service. Somewhat related to the scope of performance, the term of your agreement secures the time frame during which you are hiring the services of the promotions company. This may vary based on which service you are contracting. For example, a publicist or web-marketing firm may be hired for a specific number of months to ramp up a campaign; thereafter, depending on the success and momentum of the campaign, they may be extended on a month-to-month basis. A radio promoter might be hired for the entire "radio cycle" of a single—the time it takes it to reach a peak chart position or number of stations playing it and then gradually backing off to minimal airplay. Depending on how the single catches on with radio stations and the public, this period of time could last for weeks or months.

Fees and costs. These vary widely based on the service given, so it is important that you first do your homework by shopping around, comparing prices, and seeing if the person you are hiring is providing their service at a competitive fee. Clearly establish what is included in the price you are quoted based on the scope of performance that you have agreed on. Be very clear what costs are going to be added to the fees and when those costs are added to the fees. Negotiate benchmarks and specific goals that are tied into payments and bonuses, if possible. Sometimes promotions companies will ask for advance payments of costs. If so, make sure that the costs are placed in a separate account, require your approval, are accounted for, and if not spent, will be returned to you.

Restrictions on service. You may consider restricting certain acts or vice versa. For example, you might want to specify that a radio promoter will not commit any acts that may violate any payola or plugola laws while promoting your project, or that a street team will not deface any public property when hanging posters or harass the public when handing out flyers for you. Conversely, a publicist may reserve the right to stop representing you if you were to commit a felony or were associated with public drunkenness or drug use.

Follow up. During a promotions campaign and when a promotions campaign has ended, periodic progress reports would be helpful. If contacts are made on your behalf, it is important to establish who is going to be responsible for following up with these contacts. If there are any specific tasks to be performed after the term of the agreement or beyond the scope of the agreement, be clear who will do it.

Above all else, be realistic with your promotions campaign. A publicist cannot create your story or make a publication give you a good review. You have to do something compelling, and your art has to be competitive. Just because you hired someone to promote you, don't back off from gigging, answering e-mails and fan mail from your fans, continuing to create music, and developing your network of industry and fan contacts. Support your concert, product release, or other campaigns by cooperating with the press, radio, and other media sources. Sure, you would like your privacy, but the ticket- and music-buying public would like to know about you, as well. If you treat a reporter or DJ poorly, you never know how it might hurt you down the road. If you can be very clear about your promotions goals and enhance the chances of those working for you by being the best musician you can be who continues to have an honest, heartfelt, and interesting story to tell, the agreements that you make to promote your music will be performed with honor and pleasure.

12 Care and Feeding of Your Entertainment Lawyer

*C*onsigliore: That word has a special ring to it that has grabbed me ever since I read Mario Puzo's *The Godfather* when I was in junior high school. Whether in real life or in fiction, the attorney-client relationship is often portrayed as one of the most revered relationships in the corporate world. From seeing CEOs whispering to their lawyers when testifying before Congress on the evening news to reading brilliant writers describe the relationship in novels, we are reminded that communications exchanged between lawyers and their clients are sacred because of their special relationship. The relationship is one of trust. It is one of confidentiality. It is one of sharing and caring. If it grows enough, the lawyer will earn the right to be called a *consigliore*.

Lawyer Shopping

Shopping for a lawyer can be a challenging task. You can make it easier on yourself by looking in the right places. Most cities have lawyer-referral services that categorize lawyers by specialties, including intellectual property and entertainment services. You can also look for referrals from music industry trade associations in your area. There are a variety of music industry books, directories, and professional guides that include lawyers. Some even list lawyers by specialties and what kinds of services they render such as deal shopping, contract negotiation, and entertainment litigation.

The Internet is always a great gateway to finding entertainment lawyers. Many write for entertainment publications or websites, so you can test drive their knowledge and demeanor. Attend music business conferences to meet lawyers. Even if you can't attend these conferences, you could look at their program materials to see which lawyers are participating. Many entertainment lawyers teach courses in music business. Taking the course is a good opportunity to get to know that particular lawyer or get the phone numbers of colleagues.

As with any other professional in this business, the best way to find a couple of good names is to get solid referrals from people you know in the business. Ask everyone you know for a few names and then interview them all. Be sure to ask whether they provide the services you are seeking. (For example, do they shop artists for deals? Do they work with writers/producers? Do they advise start-up record labels?) If you need them for only a single task, make sure they aren't seeking a long-term relationship. Ask where they are in their career timelines and whether their career plans and goals are compatible with yours. Choose carefully and don't be afraid to ask the hard questions to best suit your career.

Maintenance

In an effort to promote healthy attorney-client relationships, I decided to include the following checklist in this book. I've always fantasized that lawyers and musicians should each come with an owner's manual the way that high-tech equipment does, so they could better understand how to work well with one another. This list is comprised of a number of tips based on the praise and gripes I've heard from musicians and lawyers about the successes and failures in their relationships. They are listed in no particular order of importance.

Share Your Music. Chances are that one of the lawyers you are thinking about hiring to represent you got into entertainment law out of genuine love for music. One of the best icebreakers for the attorney-client relationship is to share ideas, influences, and philosophies about music and business. You are looking for an attorney to entrust with your artistry, so a short, specially prepared demo package will go a long way toward showing that you have put some effort into helping this person understand you artistically.

I like it when I talk to other lawyers and learn they have a solid artistic understanding of their clients. A very unscientific test that I employ to test lawyers' understanding of and commitment to their clients is to ask whether they can sing at least one of each of their clients' songs. It tells me that the lawyer is listening to and making an attempt to understand their clients' artistry.

At some point early in your relationship, you may want to put some time aside to listen to some music together. Most lawyers with whom I am familiar won't bill you for this "getting to know you" time, so try to be sensitive to the fact that you probably won't have time to listen to your entire collection of demos and recordings of your favorite artists. (Be sure to verify that there's no charge for this time, though.) It's a good opportunity for you to ask about your lawyer's taste in music and reasons for getting into the industry. See if you're as comfortable talking music with your lawyer as you are talking business. After all, your music is the bond that holds the relationship together.

Your Lawyer Has Other Clients. Unless you have hired your lawyer as a full-time employee, be aware that it is physically and mentally impossible to be thinking about your matters 24 hours a day. One frustration I hear from lawyers on a regular basis is that their attention to a client's matter doesn't synchronize with the client's attention to the matter. If your lawyer isn't thinking about what you're thinking about at the same time you are, that does not mean that he doesn't care. It simply means that you're just out of sync for the moment. When choosing a lawyer, get an idea of his ability to prioritize and give you the attention that you need in a respectful and timely manner. Remember that if your lawyer is a diligent one who is giving someone else undivided attention for the moment, you are likely to get the same undivided attention if you are patient.

The good thing about the intersection of music and law in our industry is that only on rare occasions is there a true emergency situation. Sometimes quick decisions will need to be made, such as whether part of a nationally televised performance will be considered obscene, but it's not like criminal law, where lawyers need to be available constantly for clients in relatively dire situations. A good guideline for determining whether you have a good match with your lawyer is to see whether your lawyer is constantly in a state of emergency—taking other calls, constantly hurrying, always working on "the big deal." If that deal is your deal, I suppose that you would be more understanding, but if it never seems to be your deal or matter, perhaps it's time to move on.

Be Willing to Pay for the Work. Contrary to popular belief, not every lawyer is a millionaire. Perhaps it's the media, perhaps it's our collective imaginations, perhaps it's simply a misunderstanding of how the law business works, but I will repeat once again: Not every lawyer is a millionaire. This notion is just as wild a fantasy as thinking that all musicians are millionaires. Ask 20 musicians you know whether they made a million bucks last year and you are likely to dispel that rumor. The same goes for entertainment lawyers. The media and our culture have a bad habit of highlighting the rich and famous of the world, including music stars and the people who represent them. I know a lot of entertainment lawyers. It's just like any other industry: Some make a lot of money, some are barely squeaking by. It is neither realistic nor respectful to assume that a lawyer can afford to work for you for free because all lawyers are rolling in wealth. I would no sooner ask you to play a high school prom for free because I read in the newspaper that the top-10-grossing concert tours made a billion dollars last year.

I am enough of a realist to know that you might not be able to pay $500 an hour for advice. It is important to understand the distinction between being willing to pay and being able to pay. The unwillingness to pay is just not a basis for a healthy relationship. The good news is that you have options if you can't afford to spend a lot of money. Many cities have organizations that refer clients to affiliated lawyers on a no-fee or low-fee basis depending on the financial status of the client. Many lawyers are willing to set up payment plans, do their work on a percentage basis, or even speculate their fees much like a recording studio would. My only caution in the last two examples is that a lawyer who is depending on you to agree to a deal in order to get paid is less likely to tell you that you should walk away from the deal. I am not trying to imply any kind of deceit or "inside industry" dealings, it's just the logical reality of a business relationship.

Your Lawyer Doesn't Make Your Demo Any Better. I'm repeating this from my introductory chapter of this book, but I cannot stress it enough. When you hire a lawyer or other representative—especially if it is to shop you around to the industry in an effort to find you some sort of deal—your representatives cannot make your artistry any better than it is. True, some lawyers have access to many more opportunities than you because of their experience, but give some thought to where that experience and access came from. It came from representing great talent. If you are hiring the same lawyer who represented someone who is already rich, famous, and gifted, that doesn't mean that you are automatically of the same status. You still will have to prove yourself when the time comes.

Conversely, if your lawyer can't get a deal for you, it might not necessarily be the lawyer's fault. I've heard artists completely trash some lawyers' reputations for having "no clout" or for being weak simply because the record labels were not jumping at signing a project. This completely discounts whether a particular label already has an act like that artist and is in no need for another one, what the signing power of the lawyer's contacts at that label was at the time, and whether the demo was any good. Don't be discouraged and don't assume that getting in the door is the final step to your success.

Don't Hide Behind Your Lawyer. Often, musicians will hire a lawyer to talk for them simply to avoid confrontation. While this is a good practice when advice, objectivity, and detachment from personalities or a volatile situation is necessary, it can turn into a high-priced game of "chicken" when the parties really need to talk to each other. Intimate relationships like songwriting or making memorable recordings that break up sometimes need to have a spirit of reconciliation or communication rather than putting up additional boundaries, like lawyers doing the talking for you. For example, hundreds if not thousands of dollars can be spent on an ongoing correspondence between lawyers trying to "negotiate" the difference between a 5 percent disagreement on the co-writing split of a song if two artists are unwilling to talk to each other. The more practical, prudent, and logical solution would be to pick up the phone and talk.

Take Responsibility for Your Career Decisions. This means knowing enough about the business to make the decisions that you need to make. It also means that you must have the courage and the willingness to say no to a deal, knowing that you can create the opportunity to get a deal you are willing to say yes to.

A business term that is overused to a fault these days is *renegotiation*. Everyone seems to go into relationships with the idea that they are not responsible for what they initially agreed to because it all goes out of the window if and when the money starts to flow. All parties to a deal must take the time to understand the effect that particular deal will have on their respective businesses and simply take responsibility for the deal. In my experience, when the parties are diligent in this way, the deals are executed extremely well and are mutually successful.

Specialties Within a Specialty

If you have picked up anything from this book by now, it is that the practice of entertainment law is a highly specialized field. Throughout the book, I've primarily discussed the transactional side of the practice because entertainment law is largely dictated by the various agreements and relationships between parties involved in the business.

When new issues arise for an artist, more specialists need to be brought into the picture. One way an artist can prepare for this while keeping continuity in representation is to hire a law firm that has multiple areas of practice. Another approach is to use one lawyer as a general counsel and let that lawyer distribute and oversee the specialty work as it comes up. Here is a broad overview of some of the other law specialties that musicians often require.

Taxation. A blessing and curse of the entertainment industry is that vast fortunes can be made with one hit record. Many musicians have enjoyed the high life for a fleeting moment, only to come crashing back down to earth because of the burden of taxes. Because an artist can literally be catapulted from living at the poverty level to becoming a millionaire with one royalty check, the need for experienced tax advice is a necessity.

It is wise for artists even just starting out in the business to have a good accountant to help navigate income tax issues. Tax lawyers work closely with artists' accountants to handle a variety of financial matters. One important task is to choose an artist's business entity and to locate it in a state that offers the best tax advantages. Another important role for a tax attorney is structuring when and how an artist will be paid by the record label or publishing company, as these details can substantially affect the amount of tax that the artist will have to pay. If an artist tours throughout the United States and to foreign countries, tax lawyers need to be familiar with the tax practices of the various states and countries, ensuring that the proper procedures are followed.

Criminal Law. Throughout the history of the music industry, part of the mystique of stardom is that musicians have always been renegades, breaking the rules of convention and society. For a variety of reasons, a celebrity lifestyle breeds the opportunity to get into criminal trouble and brings with it higher scrutiny from law enforcement and the media. Relatively minor offenses like being drunk and disorderly or shoving a person who is violating one's privacy are considered routine when the crimes are committed by everyday citizens. When the same crimes are committed by celebrities, suddenly the infraction is worthy of headlines and prime time news coverage.

Celebrity criminal defense requires that a lawyer have a specialized knowledge of how to defend a client while the media is watching. Some techniques may include trying to keep proceedings out of the media altogether or asking for gag orders so the artist doesn't have a trial in the media. When an all-out public celebrity criminal trial takes place, however, you can expect to see press conferences from defense lawyers almost daily. Bear in mind that when hiring these mouthpieces to represent you in court and in the media, the fees may run into a pretty penny.

Constitutional Law. Our Constitution is one of the most important documents ever drafted. It is also complex and has been interpreted in many ways throughout the years. Some lawyers have developed a specialty in representing individuals' constitutional rights.

The two major constitutional rights that artists encounter are the right to privacy and the right to free speech. As discussed previously, the right to a private life is somewhat compromised when a person in the music industry reaches celebrity status and becomes a "public figure," no matter how modest that celebrity status may be. A good constitutional lawyer can dispense solid advice on the boundaries of the press, the public, and you.

Freedom of expression is the lifeblood of artists. Freedom of expression covers a wide range of artistic issues, from whether your live act is considered obscene, to your criticism of our government, to what artwork you can use on your CD packaging. If you have any questions regarding theses types of issues and your project, you should consult with a constitutional law practitioner before proceeding so you don't put an entire promotional campaign or concert tour in jeopardy because it is not considered to be constitutionally protected speech.

Family Law. Divorce, separation, paternity, and child custody and support issues are highly charged legal matters. They are also a regular occurrence in the music industry. Often, the lifestyle of the musician is not considered conducive to what is generally accepted as a conventional family life. Long, odd working hours, being away from home for long stretches of time while touring or promoting a recording, and a partylike lifestyle sometimes can put a strain on relationships. Breakups happen, children are born from casual and not-so-casual relationships, lawyers are called.

A musician's family law issues once again require a specialist familiar with the industry. One of the biggest concerns is the issue of valuation of intellectual property and copyrights when it comes to a settlement. Depending on the timing of a breakup, the property involved (for example, present and future royalties, a catalog of songs, or rights to a movie) may be worth pennies or millions. If a musician fathers multiple children from extramarital affairs while on the road, are those children entitled to live the same lifestyle as the musician's children who live at home with him and his spouse?

Estate Planning. Another law specialty somewhat related to family law matters is estate planning for the musician. A number of high-profile artists have died at very young ages from accidents, drug overdoses, or illness, leaving issues such as insurance, wills, and trusts undocumented. Depending on the state of the deceased artist's residence, this could prove disastrous, as the property left behind could be subject to probate or estate taxes, or—even worse—never get passed to the artist's family at all.

Planning for an artist's estate once again requires that the artist's lawyer have a clear understanding of entertainment industry economics. The practitioner needs to contemplate ownership interests in the various businesses, intellectual property, and royalties that will continue to generate income. Establishing a will, medical directives, and instructions for burial; donating to charities; and designating trustees to administer future royalties—these are all part of the work for the estate planner to take into account when assisting an artist.

Personality Law. The name and likeness of an artist is one of the most valuable assets that person has. Legal specialists work to protect these rights by aggressively preventing unauthorized people and companies from using an artist's name, trademarks, and likeness for commercial purposes. Unauthorized merchandise, express and implied endorsements, and advertising using an artist's name, image, or sound are all protected by lawyers specializing in what I call personality protection law. By protecting these interests and being more selective, the artist's true endorsement is worth much more.

Crisis Management. Because entertainers and the entertainment business are so high profile and in the public eye, the specialty of legal crisis management has developed. Lawyers who are experienced in public relations are hired in times of crisis or potential crisis such as a public scandal for an entertainer or a record company experiencing a financial downturn to establish a course of action. The lawyer works with the parties involved, as well as the public relations people and press, to keep reputations, trademarks, and profits intact, both short-term and long-term.

It doesn't matter whether you have modest legal needs with one entertainment attorney to handle it all or whether you have far-flung, complicated transactions that require a fleet of specialists. Your lawyers can help you work through details and offer expert counsel, but you need to do your part by getting and staying informed regarding your business dealings. The type of client who excites me is the one who takes on this ultimate responsibility and understands the concept of developing long-term relationships in the industry. It is this client who one day seeks and indeed finds a *consigliore*.

Epilogue: Lessons Learned

I started writing this epilogue in a café in Cannes, France, while attending the MIDEM international music conference. This conference takes place over several wonderful days every January and allows attendees to share experiences, information, and music with music industry professionals from all over the world. I'm taking a break from the hustle for a couple of moments, looking at the Mediterranean Sea, and simply appreciating everything about life. It is in this setting that I am going to try to share some of the most valuable lessons about the entertainment business and life that I've learned along the way from some of the greatest traveling companions I have shared a path with in my lifetime. The lessons I've learned from them are my personal rules.

Surround Yourself with Talent

While I was in law school, I had the good fortune of taking a course in entertainment law from a practicing lawyer who, along with representing a number of entertainment clients, was the general counsel for a startup record label. He was the antithesis of the entertainment lawyer stereotype I had etched in my brain. Not only was this lawyer knowledgeable, he was calm, approachable, passionate about his work, enthusiastic about his future, and one of the nicest guys I could ever meet. The label went on to be very successful in every way imaginable.

As I progressed through law school and the infancy of my solo law practice, I checked in with him from time to time with questions and to share my thoughts and ideas on how to grow my business. One day I asked how he was able to stay so seemingly even-keeled in the industry. He told me that the key to success was to surround myself with talent and people I liked. He said that even if at the beginning of my career only 1 percent of my day was spent with talented people and the other 99 percent with people I didn't like, if I stayed on my path and persisted, eventually this ratio would turn around. He was right. It was a great lesson. Picking and choosing those you surround yourself with in the business is one of the most important things you can do for your own sanity and career. If you develop your own talent, professionalism, and integrity, you will attract the same kind of people into your life. Keep your standards really high and together you will have a lot more fun and be a lot more successful.

The Artist Is Your Access

I met another lawyer, an executive for one of the performance rights organizations, when I made a telephone call to his office. By chance, I got the executive in person because his assistant didn't pick up the telephone. I had a question about a writer client of mine who happened to have a number one song on the charts at the time. We ended up connecting and our brief first conversation went a bit beyond just a simple question-and-answer session, eventually leading to one of the first productive industry meetings I'd ever taken.

Several weeks later, we met along with the writer I was representing and the three of us hit it off very well. We conducted a little bit of business, and it led to the executive inviting me to call when I had any questions. I was not shy to ask. One day, the executive pointed out to me that the only reason he and I had the opportunity to meet was because my question on behalf of a gifted artist opened the door. Industry representatives, record labels, publishing companies, and all other industry businesses, he explained, are always identified by the artists associated with them. If I accepted this premise (which I did), he told me that as long as I treated artists with truth, respect, and an understanding of their artistry, the artists would open the doors to other artists and to opportunities. Gifted artists who understand the business and are pleasurable to be with are the keys to the closed doors of this industry.

Don't Wear Out Your Welcome

I was giving a lecture at a small college in southern California when I asked a vice president of a large entertainment entity to join me in a panel discussion. We had done business only once several years prior, working on a project that had some positive results and some negative ones. Nevertheless, we would see each other on occasion at industry functions.

When answering a panel question about connections in the business, the executive stated that he and I had known each other for more than a decade. He explained that even with our relationship I had sent him demos of only four artists in that period of time, none of whom were a fit for his label at the time I sent the demos. Some lawyers, managers, artists, and artists' "connections to the industry" send that many demos to the same executive every month. He told the audience that by not wearing out my welcome, he knew that when I sent him the next demo—just as with the first four artists—it would be by an artist I strongly believed in and that he would give it a solid listen. That's all you can really ask for in this business: someone to give your music a solid listen and give you honest artistic and business feedback. Sometimes that feedback leads to doing business with each other, and sometimes it leads to retooling the pitch and having success with another contact.

Prepare Yourself Before Diving into the Industry

I was on a run early one morning on an unfamiliar path when I hit a steep grade that seemed like it would never end. I came upon a man walking his dogs, and stopping for a moment to ask for directions seemed like a great opportunity to rest. He seemed very nice, told me that he walked his dogs there every morning, gave me the bad news that the grade went on for several hundred more yards, and we parted ways after a brief introduction.

Out of curiosity, I looked up his name while I was preparing for a lecture that afternoon. It turned out that he was a famous Academy Award–winning director who directed a few films that I loved. I returned to the path at the same time for the next week for a daily dose of wisdom. During that time, we conversed about life, business, making movies, and making music. I asked if he had one piece of advice that I could pass on in my lectures. He told me that he had honed his craft in England before coming to America to dive into the film industry. Look at the fantastic artists who really practiced hard, created their own identities, and developed their talents before bringing their art to the industry. The world will know that you've done your homework. You can develop your talent anywhere if you set your standards high and work toward them.

Keep Learning and Teach by Example

A client and dear friend of mine comes from a family of educators. She has one of the most wide-ranging and colorful lives and careers that I've ever encountered. She has received numerous awards and recognition for her work professionally and in the community. One of the reasons her career has been so long and successful is that even though she would reach certain career goals, she was willing to learn new skills. She also has a sense of the greater community and the responsibility of artists and celebrities to that community.

We talked one day about how she always thought she would be a teacher. I felt that by sharing her talent with her audience every day, she was teaching by example. I know that from working with her and listening to her artistry almost daily, I have been reminded to pursue something I am passionate about, to strive to be excellent, and to keep learning new skills to expand my horizons. On her birthday one year, I gave her an old school bell—a traditional brass one that grade school teachers used years ago—to let her know how much she has taught me by her example. Do the same with your talents; if you are sharing what you know with one person or with millions, teach by example. The lessons will come back to you every day.

Take Some Chances

I am not advocating gambling here, I am encouraging you to develop yourself as a human being, as a businessperson, and as a confident, talented artist. There is a 100 percent guarantee of success if you don't try, but do you truly want to be a success at inaction? My best friend in the music business—the traveling companion I mentioned in the introduction of this book—turned in the ultimate unsolicited demo by leaving it on a recording artist's car in a parking lot. The song was recorded, hit number one on the R&B charts, and jump-started his career.

If you have the talent, drive, will power, and capacity to keep working hard at something you love, then take a few chances. If you can objectively step back and judge your work as being ready to compete with all of the other great artists whom you admire, then why wait? People look at our industry and think that their chances of success are one in a million. They aren't...I'm not being facetious here—it's closer to one in ten thousand. Those odds are significantly better than one in a million. If you do your homework, set your standards really high, and pick your targets well, each time you let someone listen to your artistry, you have a one-in-two chance of creating an ally in your career. Don't wait for others to make your breaks for you. Make the breaks yourself, and don't be discouraged if it doesn't always go your way. Each effort that you make is a successful act.

Your Chosen Family Is Everything

When I was in law school, we had a talent show. I got together with a couple of musician friends, and along with playing some great jazz together, we became the show's house band backing up a number of singers who participated in the show. One of these singers stood out from the rest; she could really sing. She obviously had training, liked to sing, chose her songs well, and had her own style. She could seriously express herself far better than the rest of the singers. I fell in love with her, we started a band together, and to this day, we remain friends at a high spiritual and artistic level far above that of many couples who have been married for decades.

Together, this singer and I raised two children on a steady dose of love and music. As of the completion of this edition of this book, our children are both very good at expressing themselves in their own unique ways. I'd like to think that this is a function of the environment in which they were raised: Self-expression was encouraged, and they were exposed to artists who manage to function in an industry that not only encourages but rewards self-expression. I see this repeated regularly in those who totally embrace themselves, their art, and the reality that art and the "real world" of living day-to-day in the lifestyle of their choice can exist.

Returning to my café in Cannes, I once again look at the world that I have had the pleasure of experiencing. Almost 10,000 people are here in southern France because of one thing: sharing music with others who have the same love of music. I've met some of the smartest, most passionate, and gifted people anyone could ever meet through the music industry. It all started with the encouragement of this family of my choice. My family of choice, along with my extended artistic and business family, means the world to me. This is the family with whom I share my journey. I hope that you, too, find a passion that burns in your heart, and that you find the right companions to share it with, no matter how long or short your journey with them may be.

Glossary

Here are some of the most common terms you will encounter in the music industry on a day-to-day basis. The index can guide you to a full list of terms used in the book.

A&R Short for "Artist and Repertoire," this is the creative department at a record company. A&R departments scout talent, find music, and then combine and coordinate them with other creative elements such as producers, the right studios, and side musicians to create master recordings.

Administration Rights The rights to perform the business tasks associated with services and property. These rights include perfecting rights (such as filing copyright forms), entering into contracts, issuing licenses, collecting money, and accounting rights.

Advance Payments made by one party of an agreement to another party in anticipation of being repaid from future royalties. For example, record companies will often pay advances to artists for the costs of making a commercial recording. These advance payments are repaid from the eventual royalties earned from sales of the recording.

Agent A person who is authorized to represent another person in any capacity. A more legally accurate use of the term in music is *talent agent*, which is a person who is specifically and only authorized to seek and procure engagements for a performing artist. This is an important distinction because in some jurisdictions, individuals are required to be licensed in order to become a talent agent.

Aggregators Digital distribution "agents" that represent multiple labels and/or artists collectively in the negotiation of digital distribution rights to third parties.

Airplay Broadcast of music in various ways, including radio, television, and satellite radio performances.

All-In A method of payment in which the artist's and producer's fees, advances, and/or royalties are combined.

Arbitration A contractually agreed-upon legal proceeding to settle disputes. The parties involved in arbitration may use lawyers, and the proceedings take place in a court setting, but the proceedings are generally less formal than in court trials. Arbitration procedures vary by jurisdiction.

Artist Agreement See *Exclusive Artist Agreement*

Artwork Visual art accompanying audio recordings.

Back End Income to be earned in the future, typically referring to future royalty income or payments to be made upon the completion of certain events (such as the completion or eventual sale of a project to a third party).

Business Affairs Department The "deal-making" department of a business, usually made up of music lawyers or other professionals well versed in the legal issues involved in each transaction.

Compilation A single recording comprised of multiple preexisting masters licensed from various record companies that are presented in their original form.

Conduct Clause A provision in an exclusive artist agreement intended to curtail certain behavior or conduct by artists (for example, a violent felony) that may put the artist or the associated record label in public disrepute.

Copyright See *Performing Art (PA) Copyright, Sound Recording (SR) Copyright,* and *Synchronization Right*

Copyright Infringement A violation of one or more of the exclusive rights of the copyright holder.

Cover A recording or performance of a preexisting musical composition made popular by another artist.

Derivative Work A work that alters a preexisting copyrighted work. For example, taking an existing song and revising the lyrics would be creating a derivative work.

Distribution The process of getting music to the public via a variety of methods. Distribution has evolved from the traditional warehousing and shipping of "hard goods" such as CDs to stores to digital distribution of music files by computer.

Downloads Music available in the digital form via digital distribution that can be accessed and saved onto a computer.

Exclusive Artist Agreement An agreement that an artist makes with a third party (such as a record manufacturing and distribution company or a music production company) that grants the third party exclusive rights to the artist's services for a set period of time.

First Refusal Right The right of one party to match an offer made by another party.

Flat Fee A one-time non-royalty payment for services or uses of intellectual property.

Grand Performance Rights Rights associated with music used in connection with stage performances such as musicals, ballets, or operas.

Gross Receipts Total income before recoupable costs and other payments are deducted.

Independent Label A record label not owned or co-owned by a major label.

Intellectual Property Property of the mind associated with the results of the creative process. Examples of intellectual property include copyrights, trademarks, and trade secrets.

Major Label One of the large multinational corporations that manufacture and/or distribute the large majority of the music that is produced in the United States.

Manager A person who serves as the chief executive officer of an artist's career. A manager is responsible for the development and implementation of a career plan for an artist. Also referred to as a *personal manager*.

Master Recording An audio recording that is technically satisfactory to manufacture and reproduce multiple copies for distribution and sale to the public.

Mechanical License A license granted to manufacture and sell music products for the use of a musical composition on media that requires a mechanical device in order to listen to the composition (for example, CDs, vinyl recordings, and DVDs).

Mediation A legal proceeding in which the disputing parties mutually agree upon a third party to craft a negotiated settlement between them.

Merchandising Selling goods that use the images, likenesses, trademarks, and/or artwork associated with a musical act.

Net Payments Gross receipts minus negotiated deductions.

Option The opportunity, but not the obligation, for a party to take a certain action. For example, a music publishing company may be granted an option to extend an agreement to retain the exclusive services of a writer for a negotiated period of time.

Performing Art (PA) Copyright The copyright that protects musical compositions. Generally, it is the protection of this copyright that governs the music publishing side of the music industry.

Performance Rights Organizations The companies that issue licenses, collect the money, and pay royalties on behalf of songwriters and publishers for small performance rights. Also called *PROs*.

Pipeline Income Income that has been earned but not yet received.

Promoter A person or business entity that coordinates all aspects of presenting a concert or other type of live event.

Promotions Person A person who markets an artist, product, or business entity. Most music industry promotions professionals develop specialties such as radio, retail, or college promotions.

Publicist A professional who is responsible for the development and implementation of a publicity plan for an artist. The publicist is primarily responsible for generating press opportunities, interfacing with the media, and creating a "buzz" for an artist.

Publishing Agreement An agreement granting some combination of ownership, administration, and exploitation rights to musical compositions.

Record Typically, the term used for any configuration (such as CD, DVD, or tape recordings) of an audio or audiovisual recording of a musical work. Also referred to as a *recording* or *phonorecord* in many contracts.

Record Deal See *Exclusive Artist Agreement*

Recoupable Cost The monies that one party spends directly for or on behalf of an artist (such as advances, promotional costs, and recording costs) with the expectation of being repaid or *recouped* before the artist receives his or her money.

Reserve Amounts of money held back by a party paying royalties to an artist. This reserve is kept in anticipation of returns and other costs or fees that may need to be paid out on behalf of the artist.

Ring Backs Audio recordings that are played by cellular phones that can be heard by the initiating party of a phone call.

Ring Tones Audio recordings that are played by cellular phones that can be heard by the receiving party of a phone call.

Royalty Payment based on sales or use fees derived from a right, product, or service. Examples of royalty payments include payments based on record sales, airplay, or merchandise sales.

Sample All or a portion of a preexisting sound recording and/or musical composition that is used along with original material to create a new work.

Sample Clearing The process of obtaining permissions from copyright owners to take their preexisting copyrighted works (sound recordings, musical compositions, or both) and change them to make new musical works.

Small Performance Rights The right to use music in connection with non-stage performances such as radio and television broadcasts, on-hold services, and performances of music in retail stores.

Sound Recording (SR) Copyright The copyright that protects master recordings. Generally, it is the protection of this copyright that governs the record business side of the music industry.

Speculation Services provided on a reduced fee or free basis in exchange for a higher fee in the future if an anticipated event occurs, such as an artist signing a major label contract.

Statutory Rate The prescribed mechanical license rate from the copyright law.

Streaming Music being played, but not downloaded, on line.

Synchronization Rights The rights (commonly referred to as *sync rights*) associated with the synchronization of music to visual images. Examples include the use of music in movies, on television, and in video productions.

Term Agreement An agreement binding one party to another exclusively over a defined period of time rather than according to the number of product units sold.

Tour Support Money or other financial support paid by a company in connection with touring, usually to promote a product. Tour support can be paid directly to the artist or to third parties—such as side musicians, tour personnel, audiovisual companies, or hotels—on behalf of the artist.

Trademark A mark that identifies the source of goods. Examples include band or record label names, logos, or slogans that are associated with a business.

Work-for-Hire A copyrighted work furnished by a creating party at the specific request of the hiring party in exchange for payment or other consideration. The legal copyright owner of a work-for-hire is the hiring party.

Index

A

accommodations, performance agreements, 94
accounting, physical distribution, 171
"acts of God," 98
actual damages, 141
administration. *See also* management
    collaboration, 31
    mechanical licenses, 33
    writer-publisher agreement, 39
advances
    recording artist agreements, 61–62
    recoupment, 62–63
    writer-publisher agreement, 40–43
agents, 102–104
    role of, 3
aggregation, digital distribution, 174–175
agreements
    artist, 153
    artist-management, 69–87
    business entities, 118–124
    collaboration, 29–32
    commissions and expenses, 86
    consignment, 154–155
    consulting, 155
    creative considerations, 28–29
    dispute resolution, 139–147
    distribution, 156–158
    duration of, 83–84
    exclusivity, 86–87
    limits of authority, 85–86
    manufacturing, 158
    member, 118
    money, 159
    music publishing, 25–28
    NDA (non-disclosure agreement), 15–16
    non-competition, 16
    performance, 89–104
    printing, 158
    producers, 161–162
    production, 65
    promotion, 162–163, 175–177
    publicity campaign, 163
    recording artist, 49–67
    restrictions, 43–45
    reversions, 43–45
    revisions, 43–45
    sample clearance, 45–46
    single-song, 37–38
    sole proprietorships, 113
    songwriting, 25–28
    sources of income, 32–36
    studio, 165
    termination of, 84
    term of, 38
    theme variations, 43
    work for hire, 32
    writer-publisher, 36–43
airfare, 94
all-in royalties, 63
ancillary audio visual products, 99–100
appearances, 60
arbitration, 145
artist agreements, 153
Artist and Repertoire (A&R) people, 44, 54
artist-management agreements, 69–87
    development, 71–74
    exit plans, 82
    expansion, 81–82
    industry promotion, 79–81
    major contract points, 82–87
    manager commissions, 75–77
    packaging, 77–79
artist royalty, 61
artwork, 98
    self-release checklists, 154
ASCAP, 34, 44
audience, liability to, 96–97
authority, limits of, 85–86

B

back-end fees, 93
band members, hiring, 101–102

bands
    agreements. *See* agreements
    business entities, 109–124
Beatles, The, 26
"being signed," 53
beneficiaries, 133
bidding wars, 41
"big break," 80
binding arbitration, 145
blanket licenses, 34
BMI, 34, 44
booking agents, 102–104
business entities, 109–124
    corporations, 115–116
    deconstruction, 118
    joint ventures (JVs), 117–118
    partnerships, 114–115
    sole proprietorships, 112–114
business management, overview of, 4
by-laws, 118

C

calculations
    fair advances, 42
    manager commissions, 75–77
    recoupable costs, 62–63
catalogs, determining, 37–38
catering, 96
CD cover artwork, 154
chain of ownership, 26
chord charts, selling, 35
clauses
    sign or leave, 80
    sunset, 77
collaboration
    agreements, 29–32
    songwriting, 39–40
collateral, 134
comfort and courtesy riders, 95
commercially released recordings, 14
commissions, managers, 75–77, 86
commitments, songwriting, 39–40
compilation
    master licenses for, 158–159
    records, 57
concert ticket sales, 14
consequence lines, demand letters, 144
consigliore, 188
consignment agreements, 154–155
constitutional law, 185–186. *See also* lawyers
consulting agreements, 155

contingency basis, hiring lawyers, 146
contingency plans, performance agreements, 97–98
contingent payments, 93
contracts. *See also* agreements
    collaboration, 30
    exclusivity, 73
    major contract points, 82–87
    recording artist agreements, 58–59
    riders, 95–96
    rights, 20–21
Copyright Law (1976), 33
copyrights, 17–20
    artwork, 154
    filings, 155–156
    ideas, 29
    mechanical licenses, 32
    ownership, 38–39
    percentage splits, 31
    titles, 29
    writer-publisher agreement, 36–43
corporations
    business entities, 115–116
    investor fallacies, 129
    non-profit, 117–118
costs
    advances, 41
    financing. *See* financing
    lawyers, 182
    managers, 86
    manufacturing, 54
    promotion agreements, 176
    recoupment, 62–63
courtesy letters, 156
creative considerations, 28–29
creative control, recording artist agreements, 59–60
credit cards, paying back, 129
creditors, 134
criminal law, 185. *See also* lawyers
crisis management, 187–188. *See also* lawyers

D

damage assessment, dispute resolution, 141
dates, performance agreements, 92
"deal," definition of, 49
"deal point," 80
deconstruction of business entities, 118
demand, creation of, 55
demand letters, 143
de minimus no curat lex, 141

demos. *See also* packaging
    advances, 41
    lawyers, 183
    packaging, 77–79
    shopping, 79–81
    unsolicited submissions, 19
development
    artist-management agreements, 71–74
    deals, 65–67
digital distribution, 169–170, 173–175
digital rights, 33
disclosure, NDA (non-disclosure
        agreement), 15–16
dispute resolution, 139–147
    arbitration, 145
    avoiding, 147
    damage assessment, 141
    litigation, 146–147
    mediation, 144–145
    remedies, 141–143
    self-help, 143–144
    small claims court, 145–146
distribution, 55
    agreements, 156–158
    development deals, 66
    digital, 169–170, 173–175
    physical, 169–173
    side deals, 167–175
distributors, role of, 168
division of revenue, digital distribution, 174
documentation
    business entities, 118–124
    demand letters, 143
    for investors, 130–132
    releases, 160
Do It Yourself (DIY), 62
donors, 133
duplication costs, 41
duration
    of agreements, 83–84
    of manager commissions, 76–77
duration of contract obligations, 58
duties of managers, 84–85
DVDs, 78
    ancillary audio visual products, 99–100

E

earthquakes, 98
Electronic Press Kit (EPK), 77
elements of collaboration contracts, 30
emergency situations, 98
equipment costs, 41

equitable remedies, 142
estate planning, 186–187. *See also* lawyers
exclusivity
    agreements, 86–87
    physical distribution, 170
    recording artist agreements, 56–58
exit plans, artist-management agreements, 82
expansion, artist-management agreements,
        81–82
expenses. *See* costs; fees

F

family law, 186. *See also* lawyers
featured guest artist performances, 57
federal taxes, 117
fees. *See also* costs
    advances, 41
    back-end, 93
    finder's, 79
    lawyers, 182
    for licenses, 34
    physical distribution, 171
    promotion agreements, 176
filings, copyrights, 155–156
financing, 125–137
    intentions and expectations, 133–137
    music industry financial fallacies,
        128–130
finder's fees, 79
First Amendment, 14
follow-up, promotion agreements, 176–177
"force majeur," 98
formulas for fair advances, 42
fund-raising activities, 117

G

general partnerships, 114–115
Gershwin, George, 26
gifts, financial, 133
grand performance rights, 34
grantees, 133
grantors, 133
grants, 117
ground transportation, 94
guarantees, performance agreements, 92–94
guest lists, 96

H

Harry Fox Agency, 33
hiring lawyers, 179–188
hotel accommodations, 94

I

ideas, copyrights, 29
images of musicians, 14
income, sources of, 32–36
independent artist self-release checklists,
    151–166
independent record companies,
    64–65
industry promotion, artist-management
    agreements, 79–81
infringement, copyright, 19. *See also*
    copyrights
injunctive relief, 142
intellectual property, 14
    examples of, 15
    trademarks, 17–20
    unique services, 16
Internet retailers, 173
investment relationships, 134
investors, 125–137
    preparing for, 130–132

J

joint ventures (JVs), 117–118

L

labels, 53. *See also* record companies
laws
    contract rights, 20–21
    copyrights, 17–20
    overview of, 11
    personal rights, 13–14
    property rights, 14–17
    specialties, 21
    trademarks, 17–20
lawyers
    hiring, 179–188
    relationships with, 180–184
    role of, 5
    shopping for, 179–180
    specialties, 184–188
    taxation, 184–185
legal fees, 5
lenders, 134
length of agreements, 83–84. *See also*
    duration
liability
    to audiences, 96–97
    limited liability companies (LLCs),
        115–116
Library of Congress, Register of
    Copyrights, 19

licenses
    blanket, 34
    collaboration, 31
    exclusive rights, 57
    fees for, 34
    master licenses for compilations,
        158–159
    mechanical, 32, 159
limited liability companies (LLCs),
    115–116
limits of authority, 85–86
liquidated damages, 141
litigation, dispute resolution, 146–147
loans, 117
    paying back, 129
lockdowns, recording artist agreements,
    58–59
logos, 98

M

major contract points, 82–87
management
    artist-management agreements,
        69–87
    business, overview of, 4
    collaboration, 31
    crisis, 187–188. *See also* lawyers
    mechanical licenses, 33
managers
    commissions, 75–77, 86
    costs, 86
    duties and obligations, 84–85
    exclusivity, 86–87
    limits of authority, 85–86
    role of, 3, 71–74
manufacturing agreements, 158
manufacturing costs, 54
master licenses for compilations,
    158–159
Master Recording, 77
material costs, 41
meals, cash allowances for, 94
mechanical income, 32
mechanical licenses, 32, 159
    collaboration, 31
mediation, dispute resolution, 144–145
member agreements, 118
merchandising, 14, 98–99
models, releases, 160
money agreements, 159
Motown, 26, 73
multimedia, ancillary audio visual products,
    99–100

musical compositions. *See* songs
musicians
    agreements. *See* agreements
    bands. *See* bands
    definition of, 3, 4
    fees, 41
    images of, 14
    releases, 160
    side, 101–102
music industry financial fallacies, 128–130
music publishing, 160–161
    agreements, 25–28

N

names
    sole proprietorships, 113
    tour, 98
    trademarks. *See* trademarks
natural disasters, 98
NDA (non-disclosure agreement), 15–16
negotiations
    agreements. *See* agreements
    booking agents, 102–103
    contracts, 82–87
    merchandising, 98
networks, distribution, 55
new media income, 32, 35
non-binding arbitration, 145
non-competition agreements, 16
non-disclosure agreement (NDA), 15–16
non-exclusive recording artist agreements,
    56–58
non-featured performances, 57
non-profit corporations, 117–118
no-show penalties, 97–98

O

obligations of managers, 84–85
one-off deals, 56
ownership
    chain of, 26
    of copyrights, 18
    creative considerations, 28–29
    financial deals regarding. *See* financing
    writer-publisher agreements, 38–39

P

packaging, artist-management agreements,
    77–79
Parker, Colonel Tom, 69
partnerships, 114–115
patents, 15, 18

patrons, 133
payments
    contingent, 93
    issues, resolving, 93
    to managers, 75–77
penalties, no-show, 97–98
percentages
    to managers, 75–77
    splits, 31
per diems, 94
performance
    grand performance rights, 34
    income, 32, 34
    scope of, 91–92, 175–176
    small performance rights, 34
performance agreements, 89–104
    accommodations, 94
    agents, 102–104
    ancillary audio visual products, 99–100
    audience liability, 96–97
    contract riders, 95–96
    guarantees, 92–94
    merchandising, 98–99
    no-show penalties, 97–98
    personnel, 100
    promoters, 104
    schedules, 92
    side musicians, 101–102
    travel, 94
performance rights organizations (PROs),
    34, 161
Performing Arts (PA) copyrights, 17, 26
persona, protecting, 14
personality law, 187. *See also* lawyers
personal liability, avoiding, 115–116
personal property, 14
personal rights, 13–14
personal safety, 96
personnel, performance agreements, 100
physical distribution, 169–173
pipeline income, 41
planning for investors, 130–132
powers of attorney, 85–86
Presley, Elvis, 69
pressing and distribution (P&D), 168
price of products, physical distribution, 171
principal amount of loans, 134
print income, 32, 35
printing agreements, 158
private collections, 38–39
prizes, 117
producers
    agreements, 161–162
    role of, 3

production agreements, 65
productivity, 39–40
promoters, 104
promotion
    agreements, 162–163, 175–177
    artist-management agreements, 79–81
    digital distribution, 174–175
    distributors, role of, 168
    recording artist agreements, 60
property rights, 14–17
publicity campaign agreements, 163
publishing agreements, 25–28
punitive damages, 141

R

real property, 14
record companies, 53
    independent, 64–65
    responsibilities, 51–56
recording artist agreements, 49–67
    advances, 61–62
    contracts *versus* lockdowns, 58–59
    creative control, 59–60
    development deals, 65–67
    exclusive *versus* non-exclusive, 56–58
    independent record companies, 64–65
    production agreements, 65
    promotional commitments, 60
    recoupment, 62–63
    royalties, 61–62, 63–64
Recording Industry Association of America
    (RIAA), 33
record labels, 53
recoupment
    recording artist agreements, 62–63
    writer-publisher agreement, 40–43
Register of Copyrights (Library of
    Congress), 19
relationships. *See also* agreements
    artist-manager, establishment of, 83
    exclusive *versus* non-exclusive, 56–58
    investment, 134
    with lawyers, 180–184
    songwriter-publisher, 42
releases, 160
    writer-publisher agreements, 37–38
remedies, dispute resolution, 141–143
repayment, definition of, 42
responsibilities of record companies,
    51–56
restrictions
    agreements, 43–45
    performance agreements, 92
    promotion agreements, 176–177

reversions, agreements, 43–45
revisions, agreements, 43–45
riders, contracts, 95–96
rights
    administration, 39
    contracts, 20–21
    copyrights, 17–20
    creative control, 59–60
    digital, 33
    digital distribution, 174
    exclusive licenses, 57
    grand performance, 34
    patents, 15
    performance rights organizations
        (PROs), 34
    personal, 13–14
    property, 14–17
    small performance, 34
royalties
    all-in, 63
    collaboration, 31
    mechanical licenses, 33
    recording artist agreements, 61–62,
        63–64

S

safety, 96
sales, physical distribution, 171–173
sample clearance agreements, 45–46
samples, 163–165
satellite radio, 34
schedules, performance agreements, 92
scope of performance, 91–92, 175–176
secrets, trade, 15
security (collateral), 134
self-esteem, 130
self-help, dispute resolution, 143–144
self-release checklists, 151–166
    artist agreements, 153
    artwork, 154
    consignment agreements, 154–155
    consulting agreements, 155
    copyright filings, 155–156
    courtesy letters, 156
    distribution agreements, 156–158
    manufacturing agreements, 158
    master licenses for compilations,
        158–159
    mechanical licenses, 159
    money agreements, 159
    musician/vocalist/model releases, 160
    music publishing, 160–161
    performance rights organizations
        (PROs), 161

printing agreements, 158
producer agreements, 161–162
promotion agreements, 162–163
publicity campaign agreements, 163
samples, 163–165
studio agreements, 165
trademarks, 165–166
services, unique, 16
SESAC, 34, 44
session instrumental performances, 57
settlements, 144. *See also* dispute resolution
sexual harassment, 96
shopping demos, 79–81
side deals
distribution, 167–175
lawyers, hiring, 179–188
promotion agreements, 175–177
self-release checklists, 151–166
side musicians, 101–102
sign or leave clause, 80
single-record deals, 56
single-song agreements, 37–38
small claims court, dispute resolution, 145–146
small performance rights, 34
sole proprietorships, 112–114
songs
copyrights, 17–20
creative control, 59–60
ownership, determining, 28–29
packaging. *See* packaging
private collections, 38–39
releasing, 37–38
songwriters
percentage splits, 31
roles of, 3
work for hire, 32
songwriting agreements, 25–28
collaboration, 30
commitments, 39–40
Sound Recordings (SR) copyrights, 17, 26
sources of income from agreements, 32–36
specialization, physical distribution, 171
specialties
law, 21
lawyers, 184–188
specific performance, 142
speculative damages, 141
splits, percentage, 31
state taxes, 117
statutory damages, 141
studios
agreements, 165
rental, 41

submissions, unsolicited demo, 19
sunset clauses, 77
synchronization income, 32, 35

T

tablature, selling, 35
talent. *See also* musicians
development, 71–74
shopping, 79–81
taxes, 117
lawyers, 184–185
tax-exempt status, 117
technical riders, 95
television, small performance rights, 34
Temporary Restraining Order (TRO), 142
termination of agreements, 84
terms
agreements, 38
digital distribution, 173
terrestrial radio, 34
territory, physical distribution, 171
terrorism, 98
"The law does not cure trifles," 141
theme variations, agreements, 43
"360 degree deal," 66
timing publishing deals, 43
title copyrights, 29
tornadoes, 98
tour names, 98
trademarks, 17–20
artwork, 154
merchandising, 98–99
self-release checklists, 165–166
U.S. Patent and Trademark office, 15, 18
trade secrets, 15
Traditional Publishing Deal, 37
travel, performance agreements, 92, 94
travel costs, 41
T-shirts, artwork, 154

U

Uniform Commercial Code (UCC), 99
unique services, 16
unsolicited demo submissions, 19
U.S. Patent and Trademark office, 15, 18

V

videos, ancillary audio visual products, 99–100
vocalists
fees, 41
releases, 160

W

web retailers, 173
work for hire agreements, 32
worthiness, 130
write-offs, 128
writer-publisher agreement, 36–43
    administration, 39
    advances, 40–43
    catalogs, determining, 37–38
    ownership, 38–39
    recoupment, 40–43
    songwriting commitments,
        39–40

Z

zone of safety, 13